THE VEGAN COOKBOOK FOR KIDS

EASY Plant-Based Recipes for Young Chefs

Barb Musick

PHOTOGRAPHY BY ANNIE MARTIN

ROCKRIDGE PRESS

For general information on our other products and services or to obtain technical support, please contact our Customer Care Department within the United States at (866) 744-2665, or outside the United States at (510) 253-0500.

Rockridge Press publishes its books in a variety of electronic and print formats. Some content that appears in print may not be available in electronic books, and vice versa.

TRADEMARKS: Rockridge Press and the Rockridge Press logo are trademarks or registered trademarks of Callisto Media Inc. and/or its affiliates, in the United States and other countries, and may not be used without written permission. All other trademarks are the property of their respective owners. Rockridge Press is not associated with any product or vendor mentioned in this book.

Interior and Cover Designer: Diana Haas
Art Producer: Megan Baggott
Editor: Myryah Irby
Production Editor: Andrew Yackira
Photography © 2020 Annie Martin. Food styling by Oscar Molinar.
Author photo courtesy Angela Prodanova

ISBN: Print 978-1-64739-610-7 | eBook 978-1-64739-382-3
R0

For my mom. You may not have taught me how to cook, but you taught me everything else.

CONTENTS

INTRODUCTION

HELLO THERE, FELLOW CHEF! My name is Barb and I love to cook. But I didn't always . . .

When I was a kid, I learned how to make apple pie from scratch in a class at school. For the longest time, that was the only thing I knew how to make. I made it for holidays, I made it for dinner, and I made it just because I felt like it. I made it so much that, eventually, I got sick of it, so I stopped making it altogether. It was actually much later, when I decided to go vegan, that I really got into cooking. I started spending time learning about different ingredients and how best to prepare them. Most important, I learned what flavors and textures I really like, so I could focus on recipes that make my belly happy. That is my hope for you, that you'll get comfortable in the kitchen and learn more about the foods and flavors you like most so you'll want to continue experimenting and growing as a cook.

As you dive into this book, start with the basics in chapter 1. I've included tips and tricks to help make your time in the kitchen easier, safer, and more fun—then it's on to the recipes! There are recipes for breakfasts, snacks, salads, sandwiches, meals to make for your family, and desserts. Each chapter has recipes with different flavor profiles and different types of cuisine. There are 50 scrumptious vegan recipes in this book, and I hope you'll love them all.

CHAPTER ONE

YOUR PLANT-BASED KITCHEN

Whether you're new to cooking or have been helping in the kitchen for a long time, there is always more to learn and new tools, techniques, and ingredients to try. This chapter provides an overview of the basics you'll need to tackle the recipes in this book, including tools, plant-based ingredients and alternatives, and safety tips. I want you to have fun in the kitchen and make lots of delicious food for your family and friends, so let's get started!

GETTING STARTED: THAT WAS VEGAN?!

I love to cook! It's so much fun to get in the kitchen and create something tasty with my own two hands. I've been cooking plant-based meals for about 10 years, and I'm here to tell you that vegan recipes aren't much different to make than other types of recipes. There are so many tasty vegetables, fruits, and grains to try—and you just might discover a new favorite. You know what else is fun? Creating a meal for your friends or family and not telling them until afterward that it was vegan. They may be surprised, and they'll definitely be impressed with your cooking skills.

GO-TO GUIDELINES

Cooking and baking can be a lot of fun, but they can quickly become not so fun if your food doesn't turn out right, you hurt yourself, or you are left with a giant pile of dirty pots, pans, and dishes when you're done. Follow these basic kitchen rules, and you'll be on your way to delicious results:

Check the details. Before you start cooking or baking, read the recipe from beginning to end. Make sure you understand the steps and have all the ingredients and equipment on hand.

Grab an adult. Most recipes in this book require some knifework and/or the stovetop or oven, so it's important to have an adult nearby to assist you.

Safety first. Although cross-contamination is less of a risk with vegan ingredients (because you aren't handling raw chicken, for example), food safety is still important! Nondairy milk, butter, and yogurt need to be kept refrigerated. You also need to watch out for sharp knives and hot pans (keep reading for more on stove and oven safety).

Prep the area. Clean your workspace and set up your ingredients and tools before you start a new recipe. This means double-checking that you have all the equipment (and ingredients!) you'll need (cutting board, knives, mixing bowls, measuring spoons, etc.), and prewashing any fruits or veggies you'll be cutting.

Prep the cook. The cook needs to be prepped, too! Make sure your hands are washed and that you have an apron or clean hand towels nearby. I like to tie my hair back so it doesn't distract me (or get in the food!).

Clean as you go. I am a big fan of cleaning as I cook, as are many pro chefs. When you wash your dishes and tools as soon as you're done with them, it keeps your workspace clean and organized (you're less likely to misplace a tool or skip an ingredient) and reduces the amount of cleanup work you'll have to do when you're done cooking.

STOVETOP

A lot of cooking is done on the stovetop, so it's important to know how to use this appliance safely. Induction and most electric stovetops have smooth, flat surfaces. Some may glow red as a warning when they're hot. Gas stovetops have grates with an open flame when turned on. You need to be extra careful to keep towels (and your shirtsleeves!) away from the flames. If you're not sure which type of stovetop you have, ask an adult, and always be sure to follow the house rules when using it.

OVEN

Before starting a recipe using the oven, peek inside to make sure there are no baking sheets, pans, or other items in there. If the recipe calls for a certain rack position, now is also the time to adjust it (before the oven is hot). If the recipe doesn't specify a certain rack, use the center one.

The next step is to preheat the oven, giving it time to heat up while you put together the recipe. Once the oven is hot, be mindful when opening the door. You need to be careful not to burn yourself on the inside edges of the oven door and you also don't want anyone else in the kitchen to bump into it. Finally, it's always a good idea to keep oven mitts handy and remember that the oven can take a long time to cool down after you've turned it off.

TOP KITCHEN SAFETY TIPS

1. Keep pan handles turned toward the back of the stove so they don't stick out over the edge. This helps prevent accidentally bumping into them, which can cause spilled food and burns!
2. Always use an oven mitt or pot holder when handling hot pots and pans, but don't let it get wet. A wet pot holder will not protect your hands from burns.
3. Don't wear loose clothing and always tie back long hair.
4. Wipe up spills immediately, especially those on the floor that you could slip on while cooking.
5. Keep a fire extinguisher in the kitchen or nearby.
6. Never leave the kitchen when you have something cooking on the stovetop.
7. Never leave the house when you have something baking in the oven.
8. Always be sure the blender or food processor is unplugged before attempting to remove the blades.
9. Always be careful and keep your face back when removing lids from hot foods, as the steam can burn your skin.
10. Hold knives by their handles only and always be careful with the blades.
11. Always be careful when opening canned goods. The inner edge of the lid can be very sharp (ask an adult to help, if needed).

HANDY KITCHEN TOOLS

Successful chefs have good tools, and here is an overview of some of the equipment you'll need for the recipes in this book. There's no need to go out and stock up all at once, though! Make do with what you (or your household) already have and build your collection as you continue to grow as a home chef.

Baking dish: Usually glass or ceramic and rectangular in shape, this can be used for making everything from casseroles to baked pasta dishes.

Blender: This is used to mix and puree foods. It can be stationary, sitting on your counter, or a "stick" or immersion blender that you dip into your pot or mixing bowl.

Colander: This is the funny looking bowl with holes in it. It drains water from cooked pasta and vegetables so you don't burn yourself.

Dutch oven: This heavy pot can be used both on the stovetop and in the oven (like for Pizza Soup on page 56, where you make the soup on the stovetop, then finish it under the broiler).

Electric mixer: Most commonly used in baking recipes, this helps you mix wet and dry ingredients quickly and easily. A larger stand mixer works equally well for the recipes in this book, if you have one.

Food processor: One of my favorite tools! You can use it to blend, chop, dice, and grate fruits, nuts, cheeses, and veggies.

Knives: Having at least one good chopping knife is important and having a few different types is even better. There are many kinds of knives, but the most important are a chef's knife for cutting and chopping, a serrated bread knife for slicing bread without tearing it, and a paring knife for peeling, slicing, and removing seeds from fruits and vegetables.

Large pot with a lid: A very important tool, this pot is used for boiling water, making soups and sauces, and making recipes that are too large to fit in a skillet.

Measuring cups and spoons: Make sure you have a liquid measuring cup (this will likely be glass or plastic with a handle, spout, and measuring lines on the side), a set of dry measuring cups (likely metal or plastic), and a set of measuring spoons. You can't measure ingredients properly without these items!

Peeler: There are different styles of peelers and any will work to remove the tough skin from vegetables like potatoes and squash.

Sheet pan: This is a metal rectangle with a small lip around the edge. It's used for baking cookies and bar-type desserts, as well as for roasting vegetables and baking things like tofu.

Skillet: Also called a frying pan, this flat-bottomed pan with a handle is used mostly for frying and browning, but can also be used for other kinds of cooking.

Spatulas: These tools come in all different shapes and sizes, but the two most important are rubber (or silicone) scraping spatulas and flat turning spatulas. Flat spatulas are used for flipping things in a pan (like pancakes) and for moving food from a dish to a plate. Rubber/silicone spatulas are great for mixing wet and sticky ingredients, as they are designed to scrape the sides of bowls or pots.

Tofu press: This tool allows you to easily and neatly remove the excess liquid from tofu, allowing you to control the texture of your tofu (the drier it is, the chewier and "meatier" it'll be). Learn more about this on page 11.

Tongs: You'll want a pair of tongs for picking food out of boiling water or off a hot tray. They can seem tricky to use at first, but you'll get the hang of it before you know it.

STOCK UP

Let's talk ingredients! Here are some go-to plant-based foods and seasonings every kitchen should have.

PANTRY

These shelf-stable (meaning they don't need to be refrigerated) staples are always useful to have at the ready.

Canned beans: When you have a few different types of canned beans on hand, you can create all sorts of healthy, satisfying meals in no time.

Good quality oils: I prefer avocado and olive oils, along with a general vegetable oil, which is good for when you don't want a strong flavor.

Kala namak salt: Also called "black salt," this seasoning gives you the secret power to make anything taste like eggs! You'll see it in all my "eggy" breakfast dishes, like Breakfast Tacos (page 27) and Egg-Like Tofu Breakfast Sandwiches (page 26).

Nonstick cooking spray: This helps keep food from sticking to pots and pans, especially when baking.

Nutritional yeast: This is such a popular ingredient that it has a nickname: "nooch." It has a nice cheesy flavor. You can sprinkle it onto tofu or into sauces, or even use it to make vegan "cheesy" popcorn.

Seasoned salt: There are many types of seasoned salt to choose from, but I like the Italian version because it can be used on just about any vegetable.

Smoked paprika: Not to be confused with regular paprika, this version has a smoky, almost bacon-like flavor.

REFRIGERATOR AND FREEZER

These are the most useful ingredients to keep in your refrigerator and freezer for everyday vegan meals.

Frozen vegetables: Frozen vegetables are versatile and inexpensive; plus, they can be added to any recipe you want to "bulk up."

Nondairy milk: There are many kinds of nondairy milk. Once you find your favorite, keep it on hand for cereal, smoothies, and even sauces and baked treats. My favorite is unsweetened cashew milk!

Real maple syrup: It's not just for pancakes! Maple syrup works as a sweetener in all sorts of dishes—just be sure to get real (a.k.a. pure maple) syrup, not the imitation "pancake syrup." The real stuff is less processed, so it's healthier and tastes much better!

Tempeh: Using this vegan protein is a very easy way to add "meaty" texture to a recipe, and you can even make plant-based bacon, like Baked Tempeh Bacon (page 24) out of it.

Tofu (firm or extra-firm): Tofu is a protein made of soy that is easy to flavor and can be cooked in lots of ways.

Vegan butter: You can buy this in sticks or tubs (just like regular butter), and it's good to keep some of both on hand for baking and cooking.

Vegan cheese: Just like with nondairy milk, try the different options and find your favorite brand. For more information about vegan cheeses, see the guide on page 8.

A QUICK GUIDE TO VEGAN CHEESE

There are so many different plant-based cheese substitutions that even I haven't had the chance to try them all, but I do have some favorites. Here is a quick guide to help you sort through the options.

Cheese sauce: Need a quick nacho fix or something to drizzle over steamed broccoli? Try Daiya's Cheddar Cheese Sauce, or Wayfare's Nacho Cheddar with Jalapeños—both are fantastic!

Cream cheese: Tofutti, Kroger Simple Truth, and Wayfare make delicious spreadable vegan cream cheeses, great for schmearing on bagels or toast. If you're making a dessert, Daiya's cream cheese is good because it's a little bit sweet. Miyoko's cream cheese is also amazing, but more expensive than the others.

Homemade ricotta: You can whip up a quick homemade vegan cheese using tofu! Drain and press 1 (14-ounce) block firm tofu for about 5 minutes (see page 11). Place the pressed tofu in a large mixing bowl with ⅓ cup nutritional yeast, 2 tablespoons unsweetened nondairy milk, 2 teaspoons olive oil, 2 teaspoons garlic powder, 2 teaspoons dried oregano, and 1 teaspoon salt. Use the back of a fork or your (clean) hands to break up the tofu and mix it completely with the seasonings. You want the tofu broken into little bits, but not mushy. Use immediately, or refrigerate in an airtight container for up to 3 days. This recipe makes 2 cups.

Shredded cheese: Daiya and Follow Your Heart brands make excellent vegan shredded cheese in cheddar and mozzarella flavors, and both brands are pretty easy to find in stores. Whole Foods and Trader Joe's each has its own brand that is good as well.

Sliced cheese: A few popular brands that make sliced vegan cheese are Daiya, Follow Your Heart, Violife, and Field Roast Chao. Among these, flavors range from cheddar to tomato-cayenne to smoked provolone, which is an amazing selection!

PREP SKILLS

Every chef starts out learning how to hone their cooking skills and the recipes in this book will help you do exactly that! Whether you're just starting out or already have some knowledge to build on, there is always plenty to learn. Here are some basic prepping techniques essential to making delicious plant-based meals.

MEASURING

Measuring is very important, because if you don't start with the right amount of each ingredient, the recipe won't work—you'll wind up with textures that are too mushy or too crunchy or flavors that are all wrong. Here are some tips for proper measuring.

Wet ingredients When measuring wet or liquid ingredients, be sure to use the liquid measuring cup (the one with a handle and spout). The lines for measuring (½ cup, 1 cup, etc.) are printed on the side. Place the measuring cup on the counter and pour the liquid into it until you get to the desired measurement line. Placing the cup on the counter keeps it steady and allows for precise measuring. For small amounts of liquid, use measuring spoons.

Dry ingredients For dry ingredients such as flour, sugar, and oats/grains, use the measuring cups that are individually identified by their exact amount (¼ cup, ½ cup, etc.), and that often are scoop- or cup-shaped. Unless the recipe calls for the ingredient to be "packed" (this is most common with brown sugar), you should never try to compress it in the cup. You should also use a straight edge, like the back of a table knife, to scrape along the top to make sure the measuring cup is full but level, with no extra mounding on top. The same goes for measuring spoons; you don't want the ingredients to be rounded at the top.

Other ingredients What about ingredients that aren't exactly dry or liquid, like almond butter or coconut oil? For small amounts of these ingredients, use measuring spoons and an additional spoon or butter knife to help scrape the sticky butter or oil into your mixing bowl. For larger amounts, use your dry measuring cups, along with a butter knife or scraper to make sure it all ends up in the mixing bowl or pan.

CHOPPING AND SLICING

If you don't feel confident with a knife yet, don't worry. It takes practice and you'll definitely get better at it the more you cook. The key is to go slowly, keep your eye on the knife, and be careful. To stay safe when using knives in the kitchen, it is important to use them correctly. Learning basic knife skills will make you a better cook *and* keep your fingers safe!

Knife safety tips

Keep a steady grip. It's important to have a firm, steady grip on the handle of the knife. This gives you more control while you're chopping and slicing, and helps ensure that the knife doesn't accidentally slip or drop.

Watch your fingers. While one hand is holding the knife, the other hand will be holding the ingredients. You should always curl your fingers back in and under when holding ingredients to be chopped, almost like making a claw.

Basic cutting techniques

Chop. Cut the ingredient into bite-size pieces, about the size of a nickel. "Finely chopped" means the food is cut into pieces smaller than bite size, yet still larger than diced.

Dice. Cut food into small, square pieces that are still large enough to be identified.

Mince. Cut food into tiny pieces. This cut often requires taking a second or third pass with your knife. If there is a large amount of food that needs to be minced, it can be quicker and easier to use a food processor.

Slice. Hold the piece of food firmly on a cutting board with one hand (fingers curled back and under) and then, with the other hand, use a knife to cut straight down through the food or use a sawing motion to make thin slices (the shape will depend on the food you are slicing).

PRESSING TOFU

When it comes to mastering the art of plant-based cooking, learning how to press tofu is just as important as learning how to properly measure and chop vegetables and other ingredients. Why? Because to get flavor *into* your tofu, you first have to get the water *out*. You'll notice that the recipes in this book that use tofu call for it to be "well pressed." There are two main ways of doing this.

Do it yourself

You can press tofu with items you have around the house. Start by cutting the tofu into smaller, thinner slices as called for in the recipe (or just cut it once through the middle, creating two thinner rectangles). Use a piece of paper towel to pat the tofu dry. Place a clean, folded kitchen towel on a cutting board, then put a double layer of paper towels on top. Arrange the tofu pieces in a single layer on the paper towels, then top with another double layer of paper towels and another clean kitchen towel. Top with a second cutting board. If you like, you can carefully place a book or other heavy item on top of the second cutting board—just be careful not to add anything too heavy or the tofu will get smashed, not pressed. Let the tofu press for 30 minutes to 1 hour, changing the paper towels and kitchen towels if they get soaked.

Use a tofu press

For less than $30, you (or your adult helper) can buy a tofu press online that will make it easy to squeeze unwanted liquid from a block of tofu in minutes. This allows you, then, to add the flavor you want to the tofu, either with a marinade or by allowing the tofu to soak up a sauce while cooking. There are different brands, materials, and price points to choose from.

MORE FOOD PREPPING TECHNIQUES

In addition to cutting and measuring, there are additional skills home chefs should have. Here are just a few I think you'll find helpful.

Folding Gently adding an ingredient to your mixture by using a spoon or spatula to scoop the mixture up from the bottom of the bowl and over the new ingredient just until that ingredient is incorporated.

Grating Shredding an ingredient into much smaller pieces. This can be done with a box grater, food processor, or handheld zester.

Mixing Combining multiple ingredients, usually in a bowl with a spoon or maybe in a blender or food processor. It's important to make sure everything is completely mixed and you don't see any chunks of an ingredient left (unless it says otherwise in the recipe).

Peeling Removing the skin from a fruit or veggie, usually with a peeler tool.

FREQUENTLY ASKED QUESTIONS

Here are answers to some questions and problems that might come up as you learn how to cook for yourself and your family.

What if I accidentally add too much of an ingredient?
Check with an adult first to be sure, but usually you'll have to start over again. This is why it's important to read the entire recipe before you start cooking and measure all the ingredients carefully.

Do I have to add the ingredients in a specific order? What happens if I don't?
Most recipes need to be followed the way they're written. This is especially true in baking, where not following the recipe could ruin the dish. In cooking, not following the recipe can change the flavor or change the dish altogether.

How do we know which ingredients and flavors go well together?
Some combinations are well known (like peanut butter and chocolate, or tomatoes and basil), but others may be discovered by experimenting.

Is there a difference between dry and liquid measuring cups?

Yes. Although their sizes may look the same, liquid measuring cups are best for liquid ingredients and dry measuring cups are best for dry ingredients. Liquid measuring cups generally have handles and spouts and measuring lines on the sides. This makes it easy for you to place the cup on the counter, pour in the ingredient you're measuring, and look at it from the side, making sure you have the correct amount. Dry measuring cups are designed to hold an exact amount and should be leveled off at the top with a straight edge.

Why should I clean as I go?

Because it's much easier that way—and it's what the pros do! Cleaning as you go just takes a few moments, rather than having a big ol' mess to clean at the end. You'll see this practice a lot in professional kitchens, as it helps keep areas clean, organized, and safe.

What if I don't like the fruit or vegetable in a recipe?

Swap it for something you like more! Use the same amount of the new ingredient and/or cut it to the same size indicated for the ingredient you're swapping out. For example, if you don't like the mushrooms called for in Pizza Soup (page 56), add more diced bell pepper, or whatever else you like on your pizza!

What does "season to taste" mean?

Some people like their food spicier or saltier or sweeter than others, so the recipes in this book keep ingredients like salt, sugar, and hot spices and sauces to a minimum. This means it's up to you if you want to add more. You should always add a little at a time, though, because once it's in there, you can't take it out!

Do I really need to press the tofu?

Yes. If you don't remove the excess water the tofu comes packed in, the tofu will be soft and mushy. See the instructions for pressing tofu on page 11. The exception to this is tofu you buy already seasoned and baked.

VEGAN SUBSTITUTIONS

There are so many easy-to-find plant-based substitutes for cooks and bakers today! Here's what to reach for whenever you're craving a non-vegan food.

USE THIS	. . . INSTEAD OF THIS
Almond, cashew, coconut, or soy milk	Dairy milk
Crumbled tofu or soaked cashews	Ricotta
Store-bought brands like Follow Your Heart, Field Roast Chao, and Daiya	Sliced and shredded cheese
Tofu seasoned with kala namak salt	Scrambled eggs
¼ cup unsweetened applesauce	1 egg (in baking)
1 banana, smashed	1 egg (in baking)
Store-bought egg substitutes like Follow Your Heart Vegan Egg and Just Egg	Eggs in cooking and baking
Store-bought vegan mayonnaise, yogurt, and butter	Standard mayonnaise, yogurt, and butter
Real maple syrup	Honey

ABOUT THE RECIPES

I know you're wondering what kinds of recipes are in this book, and the answer is . . . a whole bunch of different kinds! I enjoy cooking and eating a wide variety of flavors and textures, so that's what I included here. The ingredients are mostly common ones you may already have in your refrigerator or pantry, and all are easy to find in the grocery store. I've also included detailed instructions for each recipe that are easy to follow. I know you're ready to get started, so let me share some of my very favorite recipes with you! If you're looking for a quick and tasty snack, try the Creamy Buffalo Cauliflower Dip on page 47. If you're planning to cook dinner for your friends or family for the first time, I highly recommend the Creamy Bacon and Pea Pasta on page 87; it's easy, and no one will believe it's vegan! And my favorite dessert? Definitely the PB&J Ice Cream Pie on page 115—no cooking required!

LABELS

You'll notice that each recipe has labels to help you easily identify different features and choose the right one for you.

5-Ingredient Recipes with this label call for five or fewer ingredients (not counting salt, pepper, and oil), so they're usually quick and easy, too.

30 Minutes These recipes take 30 minutes or less from start to finish, so they're good for whipping up a masterpiece in a flash.

Gluten-Free These recipes are made with all gluten-free ingredients. Just watch out for sneaky ingredients like soy sauce, which, depending on the brand you buy, may contain gluten.

Nut-Free These recipes (and their ingredients) contain no nuts. Be sure not to use a nut-based milk if you're feeding anyone with a nut allergy!

One Pot If you don't want a lot of dishes to wash, then look for this label! One-pot recipes only use (you guessed it!) one pot, pan, or baking dish for cooking.

TIPS

Most recipes also include special tips to help you become a better cook, learn about ingredients, and make the dishes your own. There are the three kinds of tips you'll find:

Fun Fact I love learning new things and sharing interesting tidbits about specific ingredients and foods.

Getting Messy These tips address common cooking mistakes or problems.

Mix It Up Suggestions for adding or changing ingredients to mix things up a little or to try something new. These tips may also include allergen substitutions.

Yogurt, Granola, and Fruit Parfait, page 32

BREAKFAST AND BRUNCH

Cinnamon Swirl Pancakes

30 MINUTES / SERVES 4 / PREP TIME: 20 MINUTES / COOK TIME: 8 MINUTES

These pancakes are a special treat and are guaranteed to make you smile! Drawing the swirls neatly takes practice, so make whatever designs you like best. Swirls, stars, hearts—they all taste wonderful! This recipe makes eight pancakes and any leftovers can be stored in a plastic bag in the refrigerator to be reheated easily later.

FOR THE CINNAMON SWIRL MIX:

4 tablespoons (½ stick) vegan butter, melted

½ cup packed brown sugar

2 teaspoons ground cinnamon

FOR THE PANCAKE BATTER:

1¼ cups all-purpose flour

1 teaspoon baking powder

¼ teaspoon baking soda

⅛ teaspoon salt

1 cup unsweetened nondairy milk

2 tablespoons water

Vegan butter and maple syrup, for topping

1. **Prepare the cinnamon swirl mix.** In a medium mixing bowl, combine the melted butter, brown sugar, and cinnamon. Using a fork or a whisk, mix everything and make sure there are no clumps. Pour the swirl mix into the chef's squeeze bottle or measuring cup and set aside.

2. **Mix the pancake batter.** In a large mixing bowl, stir together the flour, baking powder, baking soda, and salt until completely combined. Slowly pour in the milk and water and mix just until smooth. Some very small lumps are okay. You don't want to overmix the batter.

3. **Cook the pancakes.** Heat the skillet over medium-high heat. You'll know the skillet is hot enough when you sprinkle in a few drops of water and they "dance" across the pan. Use a ladle or large spoon to transfer the batter to the pan, about ¼ cup at a time. Don't crowd the pan, only make as many pancakes at once as will fit easily (usually two or four, depending on the size of your pan). While the first side of the pancakes cooks, use the squeeze bottle to decorate the pancakes. When bubbles appear and begin to

**Measuring cups
and spoons**

**2 mixing bowls:
1 medium, 1 large**

Whisk or fork

**Chef's squeeze bottle or
measuring cup with spout**

Spoon

Heavy skillet

Ladle or large spoon

Flat turning spatula

pop, after about 2 minutes, it's time to flip the
pancakes. Flip and cook for 1 to 2 minutes more, or
until golden brown on the bottom.

4. **Serve.** Serve swirl-side up with butter, maple syrup,
or leftover cinnamon swirl mix!

Fruity Sheet Pan Pancakes

30 MINUTES, ONE POT / SERVES 6 / PREP TIME: 10 MINUTES / COOK TIME: 12 MINUTES

Pancakes are always a big hit and these pancakes are extra fun because they're cooked on a baking sheet as one large pancake! While they're in the oven, you can make a smoothie or clean up the kitchen so you're ready to sit down and enjoy them as soon as they're done. They're also healthy and tasty because they are made with applesauce instead of oil, whole-wheat flour, and three different kinds of fruit! Leftovers? Store them in an airtight container in the refrigerator for up to 3 days.

INGREDIENTS:

Nonstick cooking spray

2 ripe bananas

2½ cups nondairy milk

½ cup unsweetened applesauce

1 teaspoon vanilla extract

2½ cups whole-wheat flour

1 teaspoon ground cinnamon

1 teaspoon baking powder

½ teaspoon baking soda

½ teaspoon salt

1 cup sliced fresh strawberries

1 cup fresh blueberries

Optional toppings: vegan butter, maple syrup, extra strawberries, and extra blueberries

1. **Turn on the oven and prep your baking sheet.** Preheat the oven to 425°F. Line a large rimmed baking sheet with parchment paper and lightly coat it with cooking spray. Set aside.

2. **Mix the wet ingredients.** In a large mixing bowl, mash the bananas with the back of a fork until smooth. Add the milk, applesauce, and vanilla and whisk until combined (some small banana lumps are okay).

3. **Mix the dry ingredients and combine.** In a separate large mixing bowl, combine the flour, cinnamon, baking powder, baking soda, and salt. Slowly add the dry ingredients to the wet ingredients, stirring as you go. I like to use a rubber spatula for this, which helps you scrape the sides of the bowl. You want everything mixed completely, but do not overmix the batter. When the batter is smooth, gently stir in the strawberries and blueberries.

CONTINUED ▶

EQUIPMENT:

**Large rimmed
baking sheet**

Parchment paper

2 large mixing bowls

Fork

**Measuring cups
and spoons**

Whisk

Rubber/silicone spatula

Flat turning spatula

4. **Bake.** Pour your batter onto the prepared baking sheet, using the rubber spatula to spread it evenly. Place in the oven and bake for 10 to 12 minutes, or until the top is a light golden brown and the pancake is cooked all the way through.

5. **Cut and serve.** Use a turning spatula to cut individual pancakes and transfer them to plates. Serve with your favorite toppings.

Mix It Up: Replace the strawberries and blueberries with your favorite fruits!

Blueberry French Toast Casserole

SERVES 6 / PREP TIME: 20 MINUTES / COOK TIME: 1 HOUR

You may be wondering why this recipe calls for old bread. Well, there's a good reason. Bread that is a couple of days old is going to be a little more dried out, which means it'll hold together better after being baked in the coconut milk and banana mixture. Fresh bread is so soft that it gets a little, well, mushy when baked in a French toast casserole. If yours turns out a little mushy, though, don't worry because it'll still taste yummy!

INGREDIENTS:

½ loaf day-old French bread (2 days old is best)

1 banana

1 (13.5-ounce) can light coconut milk

3 tablespoons pure maple syrup

1 teaspoon vanilla extract

½ teaspoon salt

2 cups fresh blueberries

EQUIPMENT:

Cutting board

Serrated knife (optional)

Large mixing bowl

Fork

Measuring cups and spoons

Spoon

2-quart baking dish

1. **Turn on the oven and chop the bread.** Place a rack in the center of the oven and preheat the oven to 350°F. Cut or tear the bread into 1-inch cubes (it doesn't need to be exact). You want 7 rounded cups, which is about ½ loaf.

2. **Mix the ingredients.** In a large mixing bowl, mash the banana using the back of a fork, then mix in the coconut milk, maple syrup, vanilla, and salt. Add the bread cubes and blueberries. Gently stir to mix. You don't want the bread cubes to break apart too much.

3. **Bake the casserole.** Pour the mixture into a 2-quart baking dish and bake on the center rack for 50 to 60 minutes, or until the top is very lightly browned and the inside has firmed up.

Baked Tempeh Bacon

5-INGREDIENT, NUT-FREE / SERVES 4 / PREP TIME: 10 MINUTES,
PLUS 10 MINUTES TO MARINATE / COOK TIME: 15 MINUTES

Can you have brunch without bacon? Perhaps . . . but why would you want to? If you're looking for a meat-free way to get your bacon fix, this tempeh bacon will do the trick. Serve it on Egg-Like Tofu Breakfast Sandwiches (page 26), alongside Fruity Sheet Pan Pancakes (page 21), or on its own with a side of fresh fruit. Or make it part of your dinner plans in the Creamy Bacon and Pea Pasta (page 87).

INGREDIENTS:

1 (8-ounce)
package tempeh

⅓ cup soy sauce

¼ cup real maple syrup

3 teaspoons
smoked paprika

2 teaspoons avocado oil or
olive oil

½ teaspoon garlic powder

½ teaspoon freshly ground
black pepper

EQUIPMENT:

Large rimmed baking sheet

Parchment paper

Cutting board

Knife

Medium mixing bowl

Measuring cups
and spoons

Whisk

Flat turning spatula

1. **Turn on the oven and prep your baking sheet.** Preheat the oven to 350°F. Line a large rimmed baking sheet with parchment paper. Set aside.

2. **Slice the tempeh.** On a cutting board and using a sharp knife (ask an adult for help), cut the tempeh into 2 equal rectangles, then cut each rectangle into 2 so you have 4 equal pieces. Cut each of those pieces into 4 slices so you have 16 thin slices.

3. **Mix the marinade.** In a medium mixing bowl, whisk the soy sauce, maple syrup, paprika, oil, garlic powder, and pepper until well combined. Add the tempeh slices to the bowl and let them soak for 5 to 10 minutes.

4. **Cook the bacon.** Place the tempeh slices on the prepared baking sheet in a single layer. Cover with about half the remaining marinade (save the rest for later). Bake for 8 minutes. Flip the pieces and top with the remaining marinade. Bake for 7 minutes more, or until slightly crispy.

Mix It Up: Use gluten-free tempeh and gluten-free soy sauce, or tamari, to make this bacon entirely gluten free!

Egg-Like Tofu Breakfast Sandwiches

30 MINUTES / SERVES 4 / PREP TIME: 10 MINUTES, PLUS TIME TO PRESS THE TOFU / COOK TIME: 10 MINUTES

I love breakfast sandwiches. The star of this breakfast sandwich is the tofu, a versatile ingredient you can make taste like whatever you want. In this recipe, the kala namak salt makes it taste like egg, helping create this rich, delicious handheld breakfast. If you want to cook the tofu ahead, let it cool and refrigerate it in an airtight container. Reheat when you're ready to build your breakfast sandwich. If you don't like the flavor of eggs, use regular salt.

INGREDIENTS:

1 (14-ounce) block firm tofu, well pressed (see page 11)

1 teaspoon Italian seasoning

½ teaspoon kala namak salt

¼ teaspoon ground turmeric

1 teaspoon avocado oil or olive oil

4 whole-wheat English muffins

Vegan butter, for spreading

4 slices vegan cheese

EQUIPMENT:

Knife

Cutting board

Measuring cups and spoons

Small mixing bowl

Spoon

Large skillet

Flat turning spatula

Toaster

1. **Prepare the tofu.** Cut the tofu in half across the short side, then in half again through the middle of the 2 pieces, making 4 thin rectangles. Lay the rectangles on a cutting board in a single layer. In a small mixing bowl, stir together the Italian seasoning, kala namak salt, and turmeric. Use a spoon to sprinkle about half the spice mixture onto the tofu pieces, then use the back of the spoon or your fingers to rub it in. Flip the tofu and do the same on the other side with the remaining spice mixture.

2. **Cook the tofu.** Heat a large skillet over medium heat. Add the oil and heat it until it shimmers—that means it is ready! Carefully place the tofu into the hot pan and cook for 3 to 4 minutes, or until the down side is a light golden brown. Flip the tofu and cook the other side for 3 to 4 minutes more, until light golden.

3. **Assemble the sandwiches.** While the tofu cooks, toast the English muffins, then spread them with butter. Pile on the eggy tofu and top each with a slice of cheese. Serve hot.

Mix It Up: There is no limit to the toppings you can add to this breakfast sandwich. Try Baked Tempeh Bacon (page 24) or some maple syrup, sliced avocado, or a schmear of vegan mayo.

Breakfast Tacos

SERVES 2 / PREP TIME: 15 MINUTES, PLUS TIME TO PRESS THE TOFU /
COOK TIME: 15 MINUTES

Tacos are perfect at any meal, if you ask me, as long as you have the right filling. This tofu scramble (a vegan version of scrambled eggs) is healthy and hearty, and you could even skip the tortilla and eat it out of a bowl . . . it would just be a little less fun. The kala namak salt is what makes the tofu taste like eggs, but if you don't have any, use regular salt instead.

INGREDIENTS:

1 bell pepper, any color

½ sweet onion

2 tablespoons water, plus more as needed

1 (14-ounce) block firm tofu, well pressed (see page 11)

½ teaspoon kala namak salt

½ cup shredded vegan cheese of choice

¼ cup nondairy milk

½ teaspoon red pepper flakes

½ teaspoon ground cumin

⅛ teaspoon freshly ground black pepper

4 small tortillas

Salsa, for topping

Optional toppings: additional shredded cheese, hot sauce, sliced avocado

1. **Prep and cook the veggies.** Dice the bell pepper and onion. In a large skillet over medium-high heat, heat the water until it bubbles. Add the bell pepper and onion. Cook for 4 to 5 minutes, until the vegetables are mostly soft, adding an extra tablespoon of water if the pan dries out. Reduce the heat to medium-low. Using your rubber spatula, push the veggies to the outer edge of the pan (in a big circle with an empty space in the center).

2. **Make the taco filling.** Using your (clean) hands, crumble the tofu into a small mixing bowl. When it's in nice small pieces, add it to the center of the skillet and sprinkle with the kala namak salt. Give it a stir, keeping it as separate from the veggies as you can (but it is okay if a bit gets mixed in). Add the cheese, milk, red pepper flakes, cumin, and black pepper to the tofu and stir everything in the pan together, including the veggies. Cook for about 5 minutes, stirring occasionally with a rubber spatula, letting the mixture get warm so the cheese melts.

CONTINUED ▶

Breakfast Tacos CONTINUED

EQUIPMENT:

Cutting board

Knife

**Measuring cups
and spoons**

Large skillet

Rubber/silicone spatula

Small mixing bowl

3. **Assemble the tacos.** When the tofu mix is warm and the cheese is melted, lay the tortillas on plates. Add one-fourth of the tofu mix to each tortilla and top with salsa or other toppings as you like.

Mix It Up: Crumble 4 slices Baked Tempeh Bacon (page 24) and add it to the tacos.

Cherry-Berry Smoothies

5-INGREDIENT, 30 MINUTES, GLUTEN-FREE, ONE POT / SERVES 2 / PREP TIME: 10 MINUTES

Smoothies are a fun way to eat your fruit! If you have glass jars with lids, you can make the smoothies the night before and store them in the refrigerator. Then, to get it nice and frosty, put the jar in the freezer for 15 minutes before drinking it.

INGREDIENTS:

2 small or medium bananas, peeled and broken in half

12 frozen pitted cherries

1 cup fresh blueberries

1 cup unsweetened nondairy milk

1 cup ice cubes (doesn't need to be exact)

EQUIPMENT:

Blender

Measuring cups and spoons

1. **Combine the ingredients.** In a blender, combine the bananas, cherries, blueberries, milk, and ice cubes. Close and secure the lid.

2. **Blend.** Plug in and turn on the blender. Pulse or process on low speed for 15 to 20 seconds, or until no more ice chunks remain. If you want to check, unplug the blender, remove the cover, and use a spoon to fish around for any pieces of ice. Pour the smoothie into two glasses and enjoy.

Getting Messy: Smoothie not sweet enough? It could be that the blueberries weren't quite ripe. Try tasting a berry before blending and, if you need to, add 1 tablespoon agave syrup to the blender.

Yogurt, Granola, and Fruit Parfait

GLUTEN-FREE / SERVES 4 / PREP TIME: 25 MINUTES / COOK TIME: 20 MINUTES

These parfaits are a delicious way to impress your family with a fancy breakfast that isn't too hard to make. They're fun to put together, too, and they give you room to experiment! You can change up the flavor of the granola by using almonds instead of pecans or dried cranberries instead of raisins. You can also change up the parfait by using a different flavor of yogurt, as well as different fruits. Yum! If you're making the granola ahead, let it cool completely, then store it in an airtight container for up to 3 days.

FOR THE GRANOLA:

¼ cup coconut oil

¼ cup real maple syrup

¼ teaspoon vanilla extract

¼ teaspoon salt

¼ teaspoon ground cinnamon

1½ cups old-fashioned rolled oats

½ cup pecans

½ cup raisins

FOR THE PARFAIT:

2 bananas

1 cup fresh blueberries

2 cups vegan vanilla yogurt, divided

1. **Turn on the oven and prep your baking sheet.** Preheat the oven to 300°F. Line a large rimmed baking sheet with parchment paper. Set aside.

2. **Make the granola mixture.** In a large mixing bowl, combine the oil, maple syrup, vanilla, salt, and cinnamon. Using a rubber spatula, stir to mix well. Add the oats and pecans and continue to stir until the ingredients are completely coated.

3. **Bake the granola.** Spread the granola on the prepared baking sheet in an even layer. Use the back of a large spoon or a spatula to press it into the pan. Place the pan in the oven and bake for 10 minutes. Stir the granola gently, then bake for 10 minutes more, or until the granola is a light golden brown. It will still be a little soft, but will crisp as it cools.

4. **Add the fruit and cool.** Move the pan to a wire rack to cool. Sprinkle the raisins across the top of the granola and press down one more time with the back of a large spoon or a spatula. Let cool completely before storing or adding to the parfaits.

**Large rimmed
baking sheet**

Parchment paper

**Mixing bowls:
1 large, 1 small**

**Measuring cups
and spoons**

Rubber/silicone spatula

Wire rack

Cutting board

Knife

**4 medium or large
drinking glasses**

5. **Peel and slice the bananas.** Remove the banana peels completely. Halve the bananas lengthwise, then cut into thin half-moons. Transfer to a small mixing bowl and add the blueberries.

6. **Layer the parfaits.** Set out 4 drinking glasses for serving. Scoop ¼ cup of yogurt into each glass. Evenly divide about half the granola among the glasses, spooning it over the yogurt. Evenly dived about half the fruit among the glasses, spooning it over the granola. Repeat with the remaining yogurt, granola, and fruit, then serve.

Fun Fact: Granola may taste like dessert but it's actually pretty good for you. It has a lot of fiber from the oats and can help keep you full all morning!

Breaded No-Chicken Nuggets, page 36

CHAPTER THREE

SNACKS AND BITES

Breaded No-Chicken Nuggets

SERVES 6 / PREP TIME: 15 MINUTES, PLUS TIME TO PRESS THE TOFU /
COOK TIME: 30 MINUTES

These little "not chicken" nuggets make a great snack! As with a lot of finger foods, the magic is in the dip. I like to dip mine in a spicy barbecue sauce, but vegan ranch, ketchup, or even mustard is also really good. You'll want to make sure you have plenty of space to set up your breading station so nothing gets knocked over.

INGREDIENTS:

1 (14-ounce) block extra-firm tofu, well pressed (see page 11)

½ cup unsweetened nondairy milk

1 tablespoon cornstarch

¾ cup panko bread crumbs

2 tablespoons Montreal chicken seasoning

1 teaspoon paprika

½ teaspoon salt

Optional: Sauce for dipping, such as ketchup, barbecue sauce, or vegan ranch dressing

1. **Turn on the oven and prep your baking sheet.** Preheat the oven to 400°F. Line a large rimmed baking sheet with parchment paper.

2. **Prepare the tofu and breading station.** Cut the tofu into about 30 cubes, all the same size. Set out 2 shallow bowls. In one bowl, whisk the milk and cornstarch until the cornstarch dissolves; in the other bowl, stir together the bread crumbs, Montreal seasoning, paprika, and salt. Place the tofu on a cutting board in front of you. Place the milk-cornstarch mixture and bread crumb mixture to the right of the cutting board and place the prepared baking sheet to the right of the bowls.

3. **Coat the nuggets.** One at a time, using just one hand, dip a tofu cube into the milk mixture. Make sure all sides are wet, then drop it into the bread crumb mixture. Switch hands and turn the tofu cube until it's covered on all sides by bread crumbs, pressing the cube firmly into the panko to help it stick. Using a different hand for each coating helps keep you and your workspace neat. Place each coated cube on the baking sheet.

Large rimmed baking sheet

Parchment paper

Cutting board

Knife

2 shallow bowls

Measuring cups and spoons

Whisk

Spoon

Tongs

4. **Bake.** Bake for 15 minutes. Using tongs, turn the cubes over. Bake for 15 minutes more, or until the cubes are lightly browned. Remove and let sit for 5 minutes before serving with your favorite dipping sauce.

Fun Fact: Montreal chicken seasoning is a blend of several spices. Make your own: In a small mixing bowl, stir together 1½ teaspoons dried parsley flakes, 1 teaspoon garlic powder, 1 teaspoon onion powder, 1 teaspoon ground coriander, ½ teaspoon paprika, ½ teaspoon ground turmeric, ¼ teaspoon salt, ¼ teaspoon freshly ground black pepper, and a pinch chili powder, any kind. Store in a sealed container.

Sweet 'n' Spicy Crispy Roasted Chickpeas

GLUTEN-FREE, NUT-FREE / SERVES 4 / PREP TIME: 10 MINUTES / COOK TIME: 30 MINUTES

Crispy chickpeas are perfect for snacking because they're both tasty and healthy. They're also great for snacking on the go—once they are completely cooled you can pack them and take them with you.

INGREDIENTS:

Nonstick cooking spray

2 (15-ounce)
cans chickpeas

1 tablespoon plus
2 teaspoons light
brown sugar

½ teaspoon garlic powder

½ teaspoon chili powder

½ teaspoon salt

½ teaspoon ground cumin

¼ teaspoon paprika

⅛ teaspoon freshly ground
black pepper

1 tablespoon avocado oil
or olive oil

EQUIPMENT:

Clean kitchen towel

Large rimmed baking sheet

Measuring cups
and spoons

Small mixing bowl

Spoon

1. **Turn on the oven and prep your baking sheet.** Preheat the oven to 420°F. Lightly coat a large rimmed baking sheet with cooking spray.

2. **Cook the chickpeas.** Drain and rinse the chickpeas, then pat them dry with a clean towel. Spread the chickpeas in a single layer on the prepared baking sheet and bake for 15 minutes.

3. **Mix the seasoning.** While the chickpeas bake, in a small mixing bowl, stir together the brown sugar, garlic powder, chili powder, salt, cumin, paprika, and pepper.

4. **Dress the chickpeas.** Remove the baking sheet from the oven and place it on a trivet or large pot holder. Drizzle the oil over the chickpeas, then sprinkle on the seasonings. Give the chickpeas a good stir and put them back in the oven for 10 to 15 minutes more, until they're nice and crispy. Remove from the oven and let cool before snacking.

Pizza Toast

5-INGREDIENT, 30 MINUTES / SERVES 2 / PREP TIME: 5 MINUTES / COOK TIME: 10 MINUTES

When I was a kid, one of my favorite snacks was these little frozen pizzas made on tiny bagels I could heat in the microwave. I thought they were just the greatest thing until I realized I could make my own mini pizzas on toast, only mine would be fresh, not soggy!

INGREDIENTS:

2 slices bread

2 tablespoons pizza sauce

½ cup shredded vegan mozzarella cheese

EQUIPMENT:

Large rimmed baking sheet

Parchment paper

Toaster

Measuring cups and spoons

Knife

1. **Turn on the oven and prep your baking sheet.** Place a rack in the center of the oven and preheat the oven to 400°F. Line a large rimmed baking sheet with parchment paper.

2. **Prepare the toasts.** Place the bread in the toaster for 2 minutes, or until light golden brown—about the same way you would want to eat them as plain old toast.

3. **Add toppings.** Place the toast on the prepared baking sheet and slather each piece with 1 tablespoon of pizza sauce, then sprinkle on the cheese, dividing it evenly.

4. **Bake.** Place the baking sheet on the center rack and bake for 6 to 8 minutes, or until the cheese melts.

Mix It Up: There are lots of really yummy "mock meats" in grocery stores these days, including pepperoni and Italian sausage, which are a great way to mix up your Pizza Toasts.

Spinach and Red Pepper Hummus Melts

5-INGREDIENT, 30 MINUTES / SERVES 2 / PREP TIME: 20 MINUTES /
COOK TIME: 5 MINUTES

This is a super healthy snack that is really delicious and filling—and it's even tastier if you use your favorite flavored hummus (like garlic or everything spice). If you're new to using the broiler, be mindful. It's easy for foods to burn when you're broiling them, so keep a close eye on the oven. I like to keep the oven light on so I can watch through the window. Some broilers are located underneath the oven, so definitely ask an adult for help if that is how yours is.

INGREDIENTS:

2 whole-grain English muffins

½ bell pepper, any color

2 tablespoons water, plus more as needed

1 cup fresh baby spinach

½ cup hummus

¼ cup shredded vegan mozzarella cheese

EQUIPMENT:

Knife

Toaster

Cutting board

Skillet

Baking sheet

Measuring cups and spoons

1. **Prep the ingredients.** Split the English muffins and lightly toast them. While they toast, chop the bell pepper into small bite-size pieces.

2. **Sauté the vegetables.** In a skillet over medium-high heat, heat the water. Add the bell pepper and spinach. Cook for 5 to 6 minutes, stirring occasionally, until the spinach wilts and the bell pepper is slightly soft. Add another tablespoon of water if the pan gets dry.

3. **Assemble the melts.** Place the English muffins on a baking sheet and slather them evenly with hummus. Top each with the vegetables, then the cheese.

4. **Broil.** Preheat the broiler to low heat. Place the baking sheet on the middle rack in the oven and broil for 1 to 2 minutes, checking every 30 seconds. You want the cheese to melt, not burn. Once the cheese has melted, carefully remove the baking sheet from the oven and let the melts cool for a few minutes before serving.

Mix It Up: Put your favorite veggies on top of these melts! Sliced carrot and chopped kale are two I like to add.

Chipotle–Sweet Potato Dip

5-INGREDIENT, GLUTEN-FREE, ONE POT / SERVES 6 / PREP TIME: 10 MINUTES, PLUS 1 HOUR TO SOAK THE CASHEWS / COOK TIME: 10 MINUTES

This dip is thick and creamy with just a hint of smoky heat. I love eating it with crackers, but I've also been known to schmear it on a thick piece of toast when I'm really hungry. This recipe is easy to double if you're feeding a large group.

INGREDIENTS:

½ cup raw cashew pieces

Boiling water, to soak the cashews

1 sweet potato

¼ cup water

½ cup unsweetened nondairy milk

¼ teaspoon salt

⅛ teaspoon chipotle powder

⅛ teaspoon smoked paprika

Optional: Raw vegetables or crackers, for serving

EQUIPMENT:

Measuring cups and spoon

Medium mixing bowl

Colander

Peeler

Cutting board

Knife

Microwave-safe bowl

Food processor or blender

Spoon

1. **Soak the cashews.** Place the cashew pieces in a medium mixing bowl and pour in enough boiling water to cover them. Cover the bowl and let sit for 1 hour. Place a colander in the sink and drain and rinse the cashews in it.

2. **Cook the sweet potato.** While the cashews soak, peel the sweet potato and cut it into 1-inch pieces. Cutting raw sweet potato can be difficult, so ask an adult for help. Place the chopped sweet potato in a microwave-safe bowl and add the water. Cover the bowl and microwave on High power for 5 minutes. Stir, re-cover the bowl, and microwave for 2 to 3 minutes more, or until the sweet potato is soft. Drain the water and set the sweet potato aside to cool.

3. **Blend the cashews.** In a food processor or blender, combine the drained cashew pieces and milk. Process for 2 to 3 minutes, or until smooth. Use a spoon to scoop half the cashew mix (it doesn't need to be exact) into a bowl.

4. **Blend the dip.** Add the cooked sweet potato to the remaining cashew mix in the food processor, along with the salt, chipotle powder, and paprika. Process for 1 to 2 minutes until smooth, adding the scooped-out cashew mix as you go until you reach your desired consistency.

CONTINUED ▶

5. **Serve.** Scoop the dip into a bowl and serve with raw veggies or crackers.

Getting Messy: Not all food processors are the same. When blending small amounts of an ingredient, such as cashew pieces, you need a food processor with blades positioned at or near the bottom of the bowl. If you have a mini food processor, it would work well for this recipe.

Creamy Buffalo Cauliflower Dip

30 MINUTES, GLUTEN-FREE / SERVES 4 / PREP TIME: 10 MINUTES / COOK TIME: 15 MINUTES

I love dips! They're perfect for family movie nights, after-school snacks, and sometimes even for dinner. This super creamy dip, with just the right amount of buffalo flavor, is definitely one of my favorites. If you're serving this to someone who doesn't like spice, reduce the amount of buffalo sauce to 1 tablespoon.

INGREDIENTS:

2 rounded cups small cauliflower florets

⅓ cup buffalo sauce

1 (15-ounce) can chickpeas

¼ cup nondairy milk, plus more as needed

¼ teaspoon salt

¼ teaspoon garlic powder

¼ teaspoon onion powder

Optional: Raw carrots, celery, and/or crackers, for serving

EQUIPMENT:

Large rimmed baking sheet

Parchment paper

Knife

Cutting board

2 large mixing bowls

Spoon

Measuring cups and spoons

Food processor

1. **Turn on the oven and prep your baking sheet.** Preheat the oven to 400°F. Line a large rimmed baking sheet with parchment paper.

2. **Season and roast the cauliflower.** In a large mixing bowl, stir together the cauliflower and buffalo sauce to coat the cauliflower. Spread the cauliflower on the prepared baking sheet. Bake for 10 minutes. Stir and bake for 5 minutes more, or until tender.

3. **Prepare the dip.** Place a colander over another large mixing bowl. Pour the chickpeas into the colander, letting the liquid (called "aquafaba") drain into the bowl. Set the aquafaba aside, then rinse and drain the chickpeas. Pour the chickpeas into a food processor along with 3 tablespoons of aquafaba, the milk, salt, garlic powder, and onion powder. If you don't have a food processor, use a blender. Process for about 1 minute, until completely smooth. Add an additional tablespoon of milk if the dip is too thick. Transfer the dip to a mixing bowl (use the one you combined the cauliflower and buffalo sauce in) and fold in the roasted cauliflower. Serve with raw carrots, celery, and/or crackers.

Fun Fact: The word *aquafaba* is from the Latin *aqua* (water) and *faba* (bean). It can be used as an egg substitute when baking.

Almond Butter No-Bake Snack Balls

GLUTEN-FREE / SERVES 6 / PREP TIME: 1 HOUR, INCLUDING CHILLING TIME

These little snack balls are easy to make and don't require any baking. The key is to make sure your balls are rolled tightly so they don't fall apart. You can even double the recipe and freeze leftovers for snacking later.

INGREDIENTS:

1⅓ cups old-fashioned rolled oats (make sure they are labeled gluten-free if you avoid gluten)

½ cup almond butter (such as Justin's classic)

¼ cup real maple syrup

2 tablespoons unsweetened coconut flakes

1 teaspoon vanilla extract

⅛ teaspoon salt

¼ teaspoon ground cinnamon

EQUIPMENT:

Measuring cups and spoons

Medium mixing bowl

Mixing spoon or rubber/silicone spatula

Plastic wrap

Large rimmed baking sheet

1. **Mix the ingredients and chill.** In a medium mixing bowl, stir together the oats, almond butter, maple syrup, coconut flakes, vanilla, salt, and cinnamon. Cover the bowl with plastic wrap and place it in the refrigerator for 30 minutes.

2. **Form the snack balls.** Using your (clean) hands, roll the chilled mixture into about 1-inch balls. Squeeze them tightly so they won't fall apart.

3. **Chill the snack balls.** Place the balls on a baking sheet and refrigerate for 15 minutes.

4. **Serve.** Enjoy the snack balls right from the refrigerator. Extras can be refrigerated in an airtight container for up to 4 days, or frozen for up to 2 months.

Mix It Up: If you don't like almond butter, use peanut butter or sunflower seed butter instead.

Apple-Oat Bars

GLUTEN-FREE / SERVES 10 / PREP TIME: 15 MINUTES / COOK TIME: 25 MINUTES

This is a great snack to bake on a Sunday afternoon and enjoy throughout the week. It makes your kitchen smell like apple pie! Store the extras in individual containers or keep them in the baking dish (covered) in the refrigerator and eat the leftovers cold—or reheat them in the microwave for 15 seconds.

INGREDIENTS:

Nonstick cooking spray

1 tablespoon chia seeds

2½ tablespoons water

2 or 3 medium apples, such as Gala or Fuji

3 cups old-fashioned rolled oats (make sure they are labeled gluten-free if you avoid gluten)

2 teaspoons ground cinnamon

2 teaspoons baking powder

½ teaspoon salt

¼ teaspoon ground nutmeg

1 cup unsweetened nondairy milk

⅓ cup real maple syrup

½ cup unsweetened applesauce

1½ teaspoons vanilla extract

1. **Turn on the oven and prep your baking dish.** Put a rack in the middle position in the oven and preheat the oven to 375°F. Lightly coat a 9-by-13-inch baking dish with cooking spray.

2. **Mix your chia "egg."** In a small mixing bowl, stir together the chia seeds and water to combine. Set aside. This creates an egg substitute called a "chia egg."

3. **Chop the apples.** Peel and core the apples, then cut them into smallish bite-size pieces to get about 2 rounded cups.

4. **Mix the ingredients.** In a large mixing bowl, combine the apples, oats, cinnamon, baking powder, salt, and nutmeg. In another small mixing bowl, whisk the milk, maple syrup, applesauce, vanilla, and chia egg to blend. Slowly add the wet ingredients to the dry ingredients, using a rubber spatula to scrape the sticky ingredients off the sides of the bowl.

CONTINUED ▶

EQUIPMENT:

9-by-13-inch baking dish

**Measuring cups
and spoons**

**Mixing bowls:
2 small, 1 large**

Spoon

Cutting board

Knife

Whisk

Rubber/silicone spatula

5. **Bake and serve.** Transfer the mixture to the prepared baking dish and use the flat edge of the spatula to pack it in firmly. Bake on the middle rack for 20 to 25 minutes, or until the top is light golden brown. Let cool for 5 to 10 minutes before serving.

Getting Messy: It's important to pack the mixture into the baking dish as firmly as you can. This will help keep the bars from falling apart after they're baked.

Strawberry, Banana, and Peanut Butter Quesadillas

5-INGREDIENT, 30 MINUTES, ONE POT / SERVES 1 / PREP TIME: 10 MINUTES / COOK TIME: 4 MINUTES

One of the best parts about learning to cook is making your snacks and meals exactly the way you like them. I love quesadillas—and I love peanut butter and fresh fruit. This recipe allows me to have both, at the same time! This gooey, tasty snack is really quick and easy to make and there's hardly any cleanup. If your home is peanut free, use almond butter or sunflower seed butter instead.

INGREDIENTS:

**1 small banana, or
½ medium banana**

2 fresh strawberries

**2 tablespoons
peanut butter**

1 (10-inch) flour tortilla

EQUIPMENT:

Cutting board

Knife

Measuring spoons

Large nonstick skillet

Flat turning spatula

1. **Slice the fruit.** Peel the banana and cut it into thin circles. Remove any green from the tops of the strawberries, then cut the strawberries into thin slices.

2. **Build the quesadilla.** Spread the peanut butter evenly onto one side of the tortilla. Place the tortilla into the skillet, peanut butter–side up, then sprinkle the fruit evenly across half of it. Carefully fold the side of the tortilla without fruit over the fruit-filled side.

3. **Cook and serve the quesadilla.** Place the skillet on the stovetop over medium heat. Cook for 2 minutes, or until the bottom is light golden brown and the peanut butter has started to get gooey. Using a turning spatula, carefully flip the tortilla and cook the other side for 60 to 90 seconds. Remove from the skillet and let cool for a minute or two before eating.

Mix It Up: Use a flavored brand of peanut or almond butter, like chocolate or vanilla, to change up the flavor a little bit.

Easy 3-Bean Chili, page 57

SOUPS, SALADS, AND SANDWICHES

Taco Soup

GLUTEN-FREE, NUT-FREE, ONE POT / SERVES 4 / PREP TIME: 10 MINUTES / COOK TIME: 25 MINUTES

This hearty soup is so filling and satisfying it will warm you from the inside out. I encourage you to play around with the toppings and change up the flavors. Sliced jalapeño and vegan sour cream are my favorites, along with the crushed tortilla chips! If you want to make it spicier, use hot chili beans instead of mild.

INGREDIENTS:

1 green bell pepper

½ sweet onion

3 tablespoons water, plus 2 cups, plus more as needed

1 (15-ounce) can black beans

1 (15-ounce) can mild chili beans (do not drain or rinse)

1 (15-ounce) can diced tomatoes

1 cup frozen sweet corn

1 teaspoon ground cumin

½ teaspoon garlic powder

½ teaspoon salt

½ teaspoon smoked paprika

¼ teaspoon chili powder

1 cup tortilla chips, slightly crushed (use gluten-free if you are avoiding gluten)

1. **Dice and sauté the veggies.** Cut the green bell pepper and onion into small pieces (dice). Heat a large pot over medium-high heat and add 2 tablespoons of water. Add the bell pepper and onion. Cook, stirring constantly with a wooden spoon or rubber spatula for 2 to 3 minutes, adding an extra tablespoon of water if the pot dries out.

2. **Make the soup.** Drain and rinse the black beans. Do not drain or rinse the chili beans. Add the black beans, chili beans, tomatoes, corn, cumin, garlic powder, salt, paprika, and chili powder to the pot, along with 2 cups of water. Bring the chili to a boil, then lower the heat to medium. Cover the pot and simmer for 20 minutes, stirring occasionally (be careful of the hot steam when you remove the lid). If the soup gets too thick, add ½ to 1 cup more water.

Optional toppings: sliced jalapeño pepper, sliced scallion, vegan sour cream, vegan shredded cheese of choice

EQUIPMENT:

Cutting board

Knife

Large pot

Wooden spoon or rubber/silicone spatula

Measuring cups and spoons

3. **Top and serve.** Spoon the soup into bowls and top with the crushed tortilla chips and any other toppings you like.

Fun Fact: If you add jalapeños to the soup, remove the seeds first—that's where most of the heat is!

Pizza Soup

ONE POT / SERVES 6 / PREP TIME: 15 MINUTES / COOK TIME: 30 MINUTES

If you love pizza as much as I do, then this is the soup for you. It has all the flavors of pizza, all the nutrients of a well-balanced meal, and although it's filling, it doesn't weigh you down. My favorite part is the cheesy bread on top, which soaks up the soup. It's best to start with slightly stale bread, as fresh bread will get soggy and fall apart.

INGREDIENTS:

1 bell pepper, any color

½ sweet onion

4 cups vegetable broth

8 ounces sliced mushrooms

1 (15-ounce) can diced tomatoes, undrained

2 cups marinara sauce

1 teaspoon dried oregano

¼ teaspoon salt

1 loaf day-old (slightly stale) Italian bread, cut into ½-inch-thick slices (enough to cover the top of the soup)

1 cup vegan shredded mozzarella cheese

⅛ teaspoon freshly ground black pepper

EQUIPMENT:

Cutting board

Knife

Dutch oven or other large oven-safe pot

Measuring cups and spoons

1. **Dice the veggies.** Cut the bell pepper and onion into small dice.

2. **Make the soup.** Place the bell pepper and onion in a Dutch oven. Add the vegetable broth, mushrooms, tomatoes and their juices, marinara sauce, oregano, and salt. Bring the soup to a boil, then reduce the heat to low. Cover the pot and simmer for 20 minutes.

3. **Top the soup and broil.** Preheat the broiler to low heat. Turn off the stovetop and take the lid off the pot. Lay the bread slices in a single layer across the top of the soup, covering as much of the soup as you can (it's okay if there are small spaces). Sprinkle the cheese over the bread and then season with pepper. Ask an adult to help you move the Dutch oven into the oven (it will be heavy). Broil the soup for 2 to 3 minutes, or until the cheese melts. Let cool for a few minutes before serving.

Mix It Up: Don't like mushrooms? Use the veggies you would normally put on a pizza, or stir in some faux meat from the grocery store, like vegan pepperoni.

Easy 3-Bean Chili

GLUTEN-FREE, NUT-FREE, ONE POT / SERVES 6 / PREP TIME: 10 MINUTES / COOK TIME: 25 MINUTES

When I first went vegan, I thought I wouldn't be able to eat chili anymore. Little did I know, all you need to make delicious chili are beans, some veggies, and plenty of seasonings. Canned beans may *seem* boring at first but, I promise, once you simmer them in all these amazing spices, everyone will be asking for a second serving.

INGREDIENTS:

1 (15-ounce) can red kidney beans

1 (15-ounce) can black beans

1 (15-ounce) can pinto beans

1 (15-ounce) can diced tomatoes, undrained

1 cup frozen corn

1½ teaspoons dried oregano

1 teaspoon ground cumin

1 teaspoon smoked paprika

¾ teaspoon salt, plus more for seasoning

½ teaspoon chili powder, plus more for seasoning

½ teaspoon onion powder

⅛ teaspoon kala namak salt

3 cups vegetable broth

Optional toppings: sliced avocado, crushed tortilla chips, shredded vegan cheese of choice

EQUIPMENT:

Large stockpot

Measuring cups and spoons

1. **Mix the ingredients.** Drain and rinse the kidney beans, black beans, and pinto beans. In a large stockpot over medium heat, combine the kidney beans, black beans, and pinto beans, tomatoes and their juices, corn, oregano, cumin, paprika, salt, chili powder, onion powder, kala namak salt, and vegetable broth. Stir well.

2. **Let the chili simmer.** Bring the chili to a simmer, then reduce the heat to low. Cover the pot and cook for 20 minutes, stirring occasionally.

3. **Season and serve.** Taste and add more salt and/or chili powder, if desired. Serve with optional toppings, as you like.

Mix It Up: Want spicier chili? Choose diced tomatoes with green chiles, or try adding red pepper flakes along with the other spices in step 1. Start with just a pinch and work your way up!

Fruity Spinach Salad

30 MINUTES, GLUTEN-FREE, ONE POT / SERVES 4 / PREP TIME: 20 MINUTES

This salad is summertime in a bowl. I love fresh berries and this is a great way to eat as many as you like and call it a meal. You can add other fruit, too, like fresh raspberries, sliced banana, or even chopped apple.

INGREDIENTS:

1 cup fresh strawberries

1 cup fresh blueberries

1 cup fresh blackberries

6 cups fresh baby spinach

½ cup chopped walnuts

¼ teaspoon salt

⅛ teaspoon freshly ground black pepper

¼ cup balsamic salad dressing, plus more for serving

EQUIPMENT:

Cutting board

Knife

Measuring cups and spoons

Large mixing bowl

Spoon

1. **Slice the strawberries.** Cut off the strawberries' leafy tops and throw them away. Cut the strawberries into slices.

2. **Mix the salad.** In a large mixing bowl, combine the sliced strawberries, blueberries, blackberries, spinach, walnuts, salt, and pepper. Mix well.

3. **Add the dressing.** Drizzle on the salad dressing, then mix again until everything is coated. Serve with extra dressing on the side.

Mix It Up: To make a homemade balsamic vinaigrette: In a mason jar or other container with a tightly closing lid, combine 1½ cups extra-virgin olive oil, ½ cup balsamic vinegar, 3 tablespoons real maple syrup, 1 teaspoon Dijon mustard, 1 teaspoon garlic powder, 1 teaspoon salt, and 1 teaspoon freshly ground black pepper. Seal the lid and shake as hard as you can until the ingredients are combined and smooth. This makes 2 cups. Leftovers will stay fresh in a refrigerated airtight container for up to 1 week. To make this salad a bit more filling, stir in 1 cup cooked quinoa before tossing with the dressing.

Great Big Tofu Salad

NUT-FREE, ONE POT / SERVES 4 / PREP TIME: 15 MINUTES,
PLUS 20 MINUTES TO MARINATE THE TOFU / COOK TIME: 35 MINUTES

When someone tells you that salads aren't a real meal, serve them this salad. It is yummy and filling and full of vitamins and nutrients. The real star, though, is the tofu. Because tofu has no natural flavor of its own, it takes on the taste of the marinade. Paired with crisp, fresh veggies and your favorite salad dressing, what could be better? I personally love a creamy dressing like vegan ranch or poppy seed, but any kind you like will work fine.

FOR THE TOFU:

Nonstick cooking spray

1 tablespoon soy sauce

1 tablespoon rice vinegar

1 tablespoon real
maple syrup

1 tablespoon water

1 tablespoon sesame oil

1 (14-ounce) block firm
tofu, well pressed (see
page 11)

FOR THE SALAD:

1 large head
romaine lettuce

1 red bell pepper

1 scallion

1 carrot

½ cucumber

1 cup grape tomatoes

1 avocado

Juice of ½ lime

½ cup favorite salad
dressing, plus more
as needed

1. **Turn on the oven and prep your baking sheet.** Preheat the oven to 420°F. Lightly coat a baking sheet with cooking spray.

2. **Marinate the tofu.** In a medium mixing bowl, whisk the soy sauce, vinegar, maple syrup, water, and oil to blend. Cut the tofu into bite-size cubes and add them to the bowl. Let marinate for about 20 minutes.

3. **Bake the tofu.** Transfer the marinated cubes to the prepared baking sheet in a single layer. Bake for 20 minutes. Carefully remove the baking sheet from the oven and spritz the top of the tofu cubes with cooking spray. Using tongs, flip the tofu. Bake for 10 to 15 minutes more, or until they're light golden brown and slightly puffy. Move the baking sheet to a wire rack and let cool a little before adding to the salad.

4. **Prepare the salad ingredients.** Chop the romaine lettuce into bite-size pieces and place in a large mixing bowl.

   Dice the red bell pepper and thinly slice the scallion. Peel the carrot and cut it into circles. Add the bell pepper, scallion, and carrot to the salad bowl.

Optional salad toppings:
sliced mushrooms, sliced
radishes, vegan shredded
cheese of choice

EQUIPMENT:

**Large rimmed
baking sheet**

Cutting board

Knife

**Measuring cups
and spoons**

**Mixing bowls:
1 medium, 1 large**

Whisk

Tongs

Wire rack

Peeler

Spoon

Halve the cucumber lengthwise, then cut it into thin
half-moons. Add the cucumber to the salad bowl
along with the tomatoes.

Lastly, the avocado: Cut the avocado lengthwise
around the seed (ask an adult for help). Gently hold
onto each side and twist until they separate.
Be careful not to squeeze too hard or you'll bruise
the fruit. Slide the tip of a spoon underneath the
seed, then scoop out the seed and throw it away.
Turn the avocado halves facedown on your cutting
board and peel away the skin. Cut both halves
lengthwise into thin slices, then across the slices to
dice. Pour the lime juice over the avocado and set it
aside. (You can throw the juiced lime half away.)

5. **Toss the salad.** Add the tofu cubes to the salad
    bowl, along with the dressing. Using tongs, gently
    toss the salad until everything is evenly mixed
    (adding more dressing if necessary). The thicker
    your dressing, the more you may need. Top with the
    diced avocado and toss one last time to serve.

Fun Fact: In some parts of the world, avocados are
called "alligator pears" or "butter fruit."

Southwestern Sweet Potato Salad

GLUTEN-FREE / SERVES 6 / PREP TIME: 25 MINUTES, PLUS TIME TO CHILL THE POTATOES / COOK TIME: 10 MINUTES

This salad is a southwestern take on traditional potato salad. Sweet potatoes and black beans always go well together and the cumin and lime give it a zippy taste! This salad would be fantastic to make for your next family picnic, but it's also pretty good on its own. Whip up a batch on a Sunday and eat it for lunch during the week. Whichever way you choose to enjoy it, remember it makes six servings as a side, but more like four as a main dish.

INGREDIENTS:

3 sweet potatoes

½ cup vegan mayonnaise

½ teaspoon ground cumin

½ teaspoon salt

1 teaspoon freshly squeezed lime juice

1 (15-ounce) can black beans

1 red bell pepper

1 celery stalk

EQUIPMENT:

Peeler

Cutting board

Knife

Medium pot

Fork

Colander

Measuring cups and spoons

Mixing bowls: 1 medium, 1 small, 1 large

Spoon

1. **Prepare the potatoes.** Peel the sweet potatoes and chop them into bite-size pieces. You want all the pieces to be about the same size so they cook evenly.

2. **Boil the potatoes.** Place the chopped sweet potatoes in a medium pot and cover them with water. Place the pot over high heat and bring the potatoes to a boil. Cook, stirring occasionally, for 6 to 8 minutes, or until the sweet potatoes pierce easily with a fork. Place a colander in the sink and drain the potatoes in it. Rinse the potatoes with cold water. Transfer the sweet potatoes to a medium mixing bowl. Cover the bowl and refrigerate until chilled.

3. **Mix the dressing.** In a small mixing bowl, stir together the mayonnaise, cumin, salt, and lime juice. Set aside.

CONTINUED ▶

4. **Prepare the rest of the ingredients and assemble the salad.** Drain and rinse the black beans, then pour them into a large mixing bowl. Dice the red bell pepper and celery and add them to the black beans. When the sweet potatoes are cooled completely, add them to the bowl, then stir in the dressing. (It may seem like a lot of dressing at first, but some will soak into the sweet potatoes.) Refrigerate until ready to serve. Stir one more time before you spoon the salad onto plates.

Fun Fact: Even though they are called potatoes, sweet potatoes are only very distantly related to regular potatoes. Also, in some parts of the United States, sweet potatoes are called yams, but they are actually very different from yams. Sweet potatoes have thin, smooth skin and are flavorful and moist, while yams have rough, dark skin and are often starchy and dry.

Tu-NO Salad Sandwiches

30 MINUTES / SERVES 4 / PREP TIME: 15 MINUTES / COOK TIME: 5 MINUTES

Get it? Tu-NO instead of tuna! The Old Bay seasoning gives the chickpeas that familiar flavor and I just love the little bite of sweet relish. For an extra dose of texture and fun, sneak in some vegan potato chips when you put together the sandwiches.

INGREDIENTS:

1 (15-ounce) can chickpeas

½ red bell pepper

3 tablespoons vegan mayonnaise

2 tablespoons sweet relish

½ teaspoon Old Bay seasoning

¼ teaspoon garlic powder (optional)

¼ teaspoon sea salt, plus more for seasoning

⅛ teaspoon freshly ground black pepper, plus more for seasoning

8 slices whole-grain bread

Optional toppings: mustard, sliced tomato, lettuce, potato chips

EQUIPMENT:

Large mixing bowl

Fork

Cutting board

Knife

Measuring cups and spoons

Toaster

1. **Prep the chickpeas.** Drain and rinse the chickpeas. Pour the chickpeas into a large mixing bowl and use the back of a fork to mash and break them apart. (This can be done more easily in a food processor, pulsing the chickpeas for 5 to 6 seconds). You want mostly small pieces, although a few larger chunks are okay.

2. **Dice the bell pepper.** Cut the red bell pepper into small dice and add to the bowl with the chickpeas.

3. **Mix the salad.** Add the mayonnaise, relish, Old Bay seasoning, garlic powder (if using), salt, and pepper. Stir until combined. Taste and see if you think it needs more salt or pepper!

4. **Make the sandwiches.** Toast the bread. Scoop some of the salad onto 4 of the toast pieces. Add your desired toppings and/or condiments and place another piece of toast on top of each sandwich. Cut the sandwiches in half and serve.

Avocado and Tomato Grilled Cheese Sandwiches

5-INGREDIENT, 30 MINUTES, ONE POT / SERVES 2 / PREP TIME: 10 MINUTES / COOK TIME: 10 MINUTES

Grilled cheese sandwiches are simple to make—but there is one important trick to know. If you want crisp, toasty bread and a gooey center, cooking the sandwiches slowly over low heat is the way to go. You also need to be careful when cutting avocados—even adults can hurt themselves doing this. Follow the instructions carefully, and if you need to ask for help, watch closely and make sure your adult helper doesn't do it wrong, either.

INGREDIENTS:

1 small tomato

1 small ripe avocado

2 tablespoons vegan butter (the kind in a tub works best), at room temperature

4 slices whole-grain bread

4 slices vegan cheddar or vegan white cheese

EQUIPMENT:

Cutting board

Knife

Spoon

Measuring cups and spoons

Large skillet

Flat turning spatula

1. **Prep the veggies.** Slice the tomato into thin circles and set aside. Cut the avocado lengthwise around the seed (ask an adult for help). Gently hold onto each side and twist until they separate. Be careful not to squeeze too hard, or you'll bruise the fruit. Slide the tip of a spoon underneath the seed, then scoop out the seed and throw it away. Turn the avocado halves facedown on your cutting board and peel away the skin. Cut both halves into thin slices.

2. **Assemble and cook the sandwiches.** Heat a large skillet over medium-low heat. Spread 1½ teaspoons of butter on one side of each bread slice and place 2 slices, butter-side down, in the skillet. Layer on 1 slice of cheese, 1 tomato slice, and about half the avocado slices (you may not use all the avocado, depending on how big your bread is). Add another slice of cheese to each sandwich, then top each with a second slice of bread, butter-side up. Reduce the heat to low and cook for 4 to 5 minutes, or until the bottom bread slices are golden brown. (Use the edge of a turning spatula to lift up a corner of each sandwich to check, being careful not to knock out the fillings.)

CONTINUED ▶

3. **Flip the sandwiches.** When it is time to flip, slide the spatula under one of the sandwiches, place your fingertips on top of the sandwich to hold everything in place, and gently turn the sandwich over so the browned side is up. Repeat with the second sandwich. Cook for 4 to 5 minutes more, until these bottom bread slices are golden brown and the cheese is all melted.

Fun Fact: The easiest way to tell if an avocado is ripe is to squeeze it gently. A ripe one will feel barely soft, not mushy.

Sweet 'n' Spicy Tempeh Pita Pockets

30 MINUTES, NUT-FREE / SERVES 4 / PREP TIME: 20 MINUTES / COOK TIME: 1 MINUTE

Sweet chili sauce can be found in the international aisle of your grocery store. If you can't find the Thai version, any Asian-style sweet chili sauce will work. Most of these sauces are somewhat similar, combining a thick, sweet sauce with just a hint of heat that goes perfectly with hearty tempeh and crisp veggies.

INGREDIENTS:

1 (8-ounce) package tempeh

⅓ cup plus 2 tablespoons Thai sweet chili sauce, divided

4 tablespoons vegan mayonnaise

2 carrots

12 dill pickle chips

4 individual pitas, or 2 large round pitas, halved

4 lettuce leaves

EQUIPMENT:

Microwave-safe bowl with a lid

Measuring cups and spoons

Spoon

Small mixing bowl

Cutting board

Knife

Box grater or food processor

1. **Prepare the tempeh.** Using your (clean) hands, crumble the tempeh into bite-size pieces and place them in a microwave-safe bowl with a lid. Stir in ⅓ cup of Thai sweet chili sauce. Place the lid on the bowl and microwave on High power for 30 to 60 seconds, or until hot. Set aside.

2. **Prepare the filling.** In a small mixing bowl, stir together the mayonnaise and remaining 2 tablespoons of Thai sweet chili sauce. Grate the carrots—either by hand, using a box grater, or in a food processor (ask an adult for help). Halve the pickle chips.

3. **Assemble the wraps.** Schmear about one-fourth of the mayo mixture onto each pita. Add the lettuce, tempeh, and pickles. Top with grated carrot. Stir the fillings together a little if you'd like, so there's a little bit of each flavor in every bite! Fold the pitas and serve.

Mix It Up: Want to make it a little hotter? Add your favorite Asian hot sauce (like sriracha) to the tempeh and sweet chili sauce, ¼ teaspoon at a time. Be careful not to add too much, because you can't take it out!

Fun Fact: You don't need to peel the carrots! In fact, many of a carrot's nutrients are found in the skin and immediately below it. Washing and drying them before eating is perfectly fine.

Mixed Veggie and Hummus Wraps

5-INGREDIENT, 30 MINUTES, NUT-FREE / SERVES 4 / PREP TIME: 15 MINUTES

I'm always surprised by the variety of hummus available in most stores these days. Garlicky, spicy . . . even chocolate! This recipe calls for plain hummus, as it allows the flavors of the vegetables to shine, but you can use your favorite flavor instead. (Except chocolate. Chocolate hummus would be pretty weird in this recipe!)

INGREDIENTS:

1 carrot

1 celery stalk

1 cup broccoli florets

1 (10-ounce) container plain hummus

4 individual pitas, or 2 large round pitas, halved

Optional toppings: lettuce, sliced tomato, sliced avocado, sliced vegan cheese of choice

EQUIPMENT:

Peeler

Cutting board

Knife

Food processor

Medium mixing bowl

Spoon

1. **Prepare the veggies.** Peel the carrot. Chop the carrot and celery into about 1-inch pieces. Place the carrot and celery pieces, along with the broccoli florets, into a food processor. Pulse for 6 to 8 seconds, or until the vegetables are in very small pieces.

2. **Mix the spread and build the wraps.** Transfer the vegetable pieces to a medium mixing bowl. Stir in the hummus. Spoon one-fourth of the mixture into each pita and add any desired toppings.

Mix It Up: Any crunchy vegetables you have on hand will work in this wrap. Cauliflower, bell pepper, and cucumber would all be yummy additions.

Veggie Lover's Pizza, page 74

DINNERS AND FAMILY FEASTS

Veggie Lover's Pizza

ONE POT / SERVES 4 / PREP TIME: 25 MINUTES / COOK TIME: 15 MINUTES

If you are a veggie lover, this is the pizza for you! I've included my personal favorite combination of vegetables, but you can omit anything you don't like . . . or add extras that you do, like sliced zucchini, fresh spinach, roasted red peppers, or garlic.

FOR THE CRUST:

1 (1-pound) ball refrigerated pizza dough

1 teaspoon flour (any kind is fine)

FOR THE SAUCE:

1 (8-ounce) can tomato sauce

1 (6-ounce) can tomato paste

1 tablespoon dried oregano

½ teaspoon garlic powder

½ teaspoon sugar

¼ teaspoon salt, plus more for seasoning

⅛ teaspoon freshly ground black pepper, plus more for seasoning

FOR THE TOPPINGS:

1 bell pepper, any color

½ sweet onion

1½ cups shredded vegan mozzarella cheese

¼ cup canned sliced black olives

1. **Turn on the oven and prepare the pizza dough.** Check the instructions on the pizza dough package and preheat the oven accordingly. Also, follow any specific instructions for preparing the dough. In my experience, it's best to let refrigerated dough sit out for 10 to 15 minutes before you begin working with it.

2. **Mix the pizza sauce.** In a medium mixing bowl, stir together the tomato sauce, tomato paste, oregano, garlic powder, sugar, salt, and pepper. Make sure the thick tomato paste is blended in completely. Taste and add more salt or pepper, if desired. Set aside.

3. **Chop the veggies for topping.** Cut the bell pepper and onion into thin slices, about 1 inch long.

4. **Make the crust.** Sprinkle some of the flour onto a baking sheet and spread it around with your fingertips. Remove the dough from its packaging and place it on the baking sheet, sprinkling the remaining flour on top. Still using your fingertips, gently move and stretch the dough until it covers the entire baking sheet. Be careful to keep the dough even—you don't want any thin spots that might burn. Note that some brands may direct you to "blind bake" the dough for a few minutes, before adding the sauce and toppings. Follow the instructions.

**4 ounces
sliced mushrooms**

Optional topping: 6 fresh
basil leaves

EQUIPMENT:

Medium mixing bowl

**Measuring cups
and spoons**

Spoon

Cutting board

Knife

**Large rimmed baking
sheet or pizza pan**

Pizza cutter

5. **Top the pizza.** Spread the sauce across the dough, starting with about half and adding more as needed (if you are using a smaller batch of dough you may not need all the sauce). Sprinkle about ½ cup of cheese across the top, then add the bell pepper, onion, olives, and mushrooms, spreading them evenly across the pizza. Sprinkle the remaining 1 cup of cheese on top.

6. **Bake and serve.** Bake according to the package instructions. You'll know the pizza is done when the edges of the crust are light golden brown and the cheese is melted. Carefully transfer the pizza to a cutting board (ask an adult to help). Chop the basil leaves (if using) and sprinkle them on top, then slice the pizza and serve.

Mix It Up: You can make another version of this pizza that I call the "animal lover's pizza." It uses store-bought vegan versions of pepperoni and sliced Italian sausage (I like Yves and Tofurky brands) in place of some of the vegetables.

Veggie Fajitas

NUT-FREE, ONE POT / SERVES 4 / PREP TIME: 25 MINUTES / COOK TIME: 10 MINUTES

Hooray for more handheld foods! I love fajitas because there are so many different flavors and textures all combined in each tortilla. The veggies in these fajitas are sautéed in water instead of oil, which means they will be a little less crisp than you may be used to. You can sauté them in oil if you prefer, but I think they're perfectly delicious (and healthier) this way. Load them up with your favorite toppings and serve with a salad and rice.

FOR THE SEASONING:

¼ teaspoon chili powder

¼ teaspoon ground cumin

¼ teaspoon onion powder

¼ teaspoon garlic powder

¼ teaspoon paprika

¼ teaspoon salt

⅛ teaspoon freshly ground black pepper

FOR THE FAJITAS:

2 bell peppers, any color

1 sweet onion or red onion

1 small summer squash or zucchini

1 lime, halved

¼ cup water, plus more as needed

1 avocado

8 (6-inch) tortillas

Optional toppings: salsa, chopped fresh cilantro, vegan sour cream

1. **Mix the fajita seasoning.** In a large mixing bowl, stir together the chili powder, cumin, onion powder, garlic powder, paprika, salt, and pepper. Set aside.

2. **Prepare the fajita veggies.** Cut the bell peppers and onion into thin strips, about 2 inches long. Slice the squash similarly. Add the bell peppers, onion, and squash to the bowl, along with the juice from one of the lime halves. Stir to combine. Let sit for 5 to 10 minutes.

3. **Cook the veggies.** In a large skillet over medium heat, heat the water. Add the seasoned veggies (along with any juice in the bowl) and cover the skillet. Sauté for 4 to 5 minutes, or until the veggies are tender, stirring occasionally. Add an additional tablespoon of water if the pan dries out.

4. **Slice the avocados.** Cut the avocado lengthwise around the seed (ask an adult for help). Gently hold onto each side and twist until they separate. Be careful not to squeeze too hard, or you'll bruise the fruit. Slide the tip of a spoon underneath the seed, then scoop out the seed and throw it away. Turn the avocado halves facedown on your cutting board and peel away the skin. Cut both halves into thin slices. Sprinkle with the juice of the remaining lime half.

Large mixing bowl

**Measuring cups
and spoons**

Spoon

Cutting board

Knife

Large skillet

5. **Assemble the fajitas.** Scoop the cooked veggies into the tortillas and top with the avocado and any other toppings you like.

Mix It Up: There are no limits when it comes to what you can put in your fajitas! Sometimes I add diced sweet potatoes, broccoli florets, and even black beans!

Rice and Bean Burritos

30 MINUTES, NUT-FREE, ONE POT / SERVES 6 / PREP TIME: 20 MINUTES / COOK TIME: 8 MINUTES

Six burritos may seem like a lot, but the thing about burritos is they make excellent leftovers! You can wrap the extra burritos in aluminum foil and refrigerate them for up to 4 days, or freeze for up to 2 months. Leave them wrapped in foil to reheat in the oven, or remove the foil wrapping (remember—never put metal in the microwave) to reheat them in the microwave.

INGREDIENTS:

1 (15-ounce) can black beans

1 (15-ounce) can pinto beans

1 teaspoon ground cumin

½ teaspoon garlic powder

½ teaspoon chili powder (optional)

½ teaspoon salt

1 tablespoon water

2 cups cooked brown rice (either prepared in advance or microwavable, like Uncle Ben's)

¾ cup your favorite salsa

2 ripe avocados

6 large flour tortillas

Optional toppings: chopped lettuce, additional salsa, hot sauce, vegan sour cream

1. **Prepare the filling.** Heat a medium skillet over medium-low heat. Drain and rinse the black beans and pinto beans and add them to the skillet, along with the cumin, garlic powder, chili powder (if using), salt, and water. Cook for 2 to 3 minutes to heat the beans. Stir in the cooked rice and salsa. Turn off the heat, cover the skillet, and let sit for 5 minutes.

2. **Slice the avocados.** Cut the avocados lengthwise around the seeds (ask an adult for help). Gently hold onto each side and twist until they separate. Be careful not to squeeze too hard, or you'll bruise the fruit. Slide the tip of a spoon underneath the seeds, then scoop out the seeds and throw them away. Turn the avocado halves facedown on your cutting board and peel away the skin. Cut the halves into thin slices.

3. **Fill and roll the burritos.** Place your tortillas on a work surface (you may need to work with two or three at a time, depending on how much space you have). Spread an equal amount of the bean mixture into the center of each tortilla, then top each with avocado slices and any other toppings you like. Roll each burrito by folding the sides to the center and the bottom edge up. Once rolled, place the burrito seam-side down on a plate so it doesn't unroll.

Medium skillet

Colander

**Measuring cups
and spoons**

Cutting board

Knife

Spoon

Fun Fact: Burrito is actually the Spanish word for "little donkey." It's true! In Spanish, donkeys are called burros, and some people say the ends of burritos look sort of like a donkey's ears.

Enchilada Casserole

GLUTEN-FREE, ONE POT / SERVES 4 / PREP TIME: 25 MINUTES /
COOK TIME: 30 MINUTES

I grew up in rural New England, where there weren't a lot of Mexican restaurants nearby. Probably because I rarely ate Mexican food, it began to feel like an occasion whenever I got the chance. I'm still a big fan of zesty south-of-the-border flavors and this casserole is an easy way to enjoy them.

INGREDIENTS:

1 (15-ounce) can
black beans

1 bell pepper, any color

1 cup sweet corn

½ teaspoon onion powder

1 (10-ounce) can mild
enchilada sauce

8 (6-inch) corn tortillas,
torn in half (you may not
use all, depending on the
shape of your baking dish)

1 cup shredded vegan
cheddar cheese

Optional toppings: sliced
avocado, fresh cilantro,
sliced scallion, vegan
sour cream

1. **Turn on the oven.** Preheat the oven to 400°F.

2. **Make the bean mixture.** Drain and rinse the black beans and place them in a medium mixing bowl. Dice the bell pepper and add it to the black beans, along with the corn and onion powder. Stir to combine.

3. **Start to layer the casserole.** Spread 2 tablespoons of enchilada sauce on the bottom of a 1½-quart baking dish, then top with a layer of tortillas. It's okay if there is some overlap, but try to create a single layer. Add about one-third of the black bean–vegetable mixture, followed by about one-third of the enchilada sauce, spreading each layer evenly with the back of a spoon or rubber spatula. Sprinkle ¼ cup of cheese on top.

4. **Continue to build layers.** Add another layer of tortillas; again, some overlap is okay. Press down gently with your fingertips to make sure the layers are packed in. Spread about half the remaining black bean–vegetable mixture over the tortillas, followed by about half the remaining enchilada

Medium mixing bowl

Cutting board

Knife

**Measuring cups
and spoons**

Spoon

1½-quart baking dish

Rubber/silicone spatula

Aluminum foil

sauce. Make sure everything is even. Sprinkle on another ¼ cup of cheese. Repeat one final layer of tortillas, followed by the remaining black bean–vegetable mixture and remaining enchilada sauce. Top with the final ½ cup of cheese.

5. Bake. Cover the casserole with aluminum foil and place it on the middle rack. Bake for 30 minutes, or until the cheese is melted and the casserole filling is hot.

6. Serve. Plate the enchiladas and add any toppings of choice.

Meatless Shepherd's Pie

GLUTEN-FREE / SERVES 4 / PREP TIME: 20 MINUTES / COOK TIME: 40 MINUTES

Traditional vegetable shepherd's pie can be time-consuming to make, which is why I prefer this simpler version. Using frozen vegetables saves the time and effort of chopping and dicing, which means you can make this dish quickly. I use a mix of frozen carrots, peas, and green beans, but use your favorite vegetables, like corn, edamame, or even broccoli.

FOR THE MASHED POTATOES:

Nonstick cooking spray

2 pounds Yukon Gold potatoes, all of similar size

3 tablespoons vegan butter

½ cup unsweetened nondairy milk

¼ teaspoon salt, plus more for seasoning

⅛ teaspoon freshly ground black pepper, plus more for seasoning

FOR THE VEGGIE FILLING:

1 (15-ounce) can great northern beans

⅓ cup vegetable broth

1 (10-ounce) package frozen mixed vegetables

1 teaspoon Italian seasoning

¼ teaspoon garlic powder

Freshly ground black pepper

1. **Turn on the oven and prep your baking dish.** Place a rack in the center of the oven and preheat the oven to 400°F. Lightly coat a 1½-quart baking dish with cooking spray. Set aside.

2. **Boil and mash the potatoes.** Cut the potatoes into quarters and place them in a large pot. Add enough water to cover the potatoes by about 1 inch. Bring to a boil over high heat. Cook for 15 to 20 minutes, or until the potatoes are easily pierced with a fork. Turn off the heat. Place a colander in the sink and drain the potatoes in it. Return the potatoes to the pot. Add the butter, milk, salt, and pepper. Using a potato masher, mash the potatoes completely. Taste and add more salt and pepper, as needed.

3. **Make the vegetable filling.** While the potatoes cook, drain and rinse the great northern beans. Place a medium pot over medium-high heat, pour in the vegetable broth, and bring it to a boil. Add the great northern beans, frozen vegetables, Italian seasoning, and garlic powder. Reduce the heat to low and simmer, uncovered, for 10 to 12 minutes, or until most of the broth has evaporated.

1½-quart baking dish

Cutting board

Knife

2 pots: 1 large, 1 medium

**Measuring cups
and spoons**

Colander

Potato masher

Rubber/silicone spatula

4. **Assemble and bake.** Mix ½ cup of mashed potatoes into the vegetable mixture, then transfer it to the baking dish. Top with the remaining mashed potatoes, using a rubber spatula to spread it smoothly. Season with a sprinkle of pepper, then bake on the center rack for 15 minutes, until heated through.

Mix It Up: Make the casserole with sweet potatoes instead of Yukon Golds.

Veggie Potpie

SERVES 6 / PREP TIME: 20 MINUTES / COOK TIME: 30 MINUTES

I remember eating frozen potpies we microwaved when I was little but, other than that, I don't think I ate one until I became vegan and decided to make my own. I love how rich, flavorful, and creamy the filling is. It's also fun to change up the veggies. Sweet potatoes, mushrooms, and kale are also delicious here.

INGREDIENTS:

Nonstick cooking spray

3 red potatoes

1 bell pepper, any color

2 large carrots

2 celery stalks

1 cup frozen peas

2 tablespoons vegan butter

½ teaspoon salt

½ teaspoon onion powder

⅛ teaspoon freshly ground black pepper

¼ cup whole-wheat flour

1½ cups vegetable broth

½ cup unsweetened nondairy milk

1 sheet puff pastry, thawed and unrolled

1. **Turn on the oven and prep your baking dish.** Preheat the oven to 375°F. Coat an 8-by-8-inch baking dish with cooking spray.

2. **Chop the veggies.** Cut the potatoes and bell pepper into large (½-inch) dice. Cut the carrots into circles and the celery into half-moons. Take the peas from the freezer and set aside.

3. **Cook the veggies.** In a large skillet over medium-low heat, melt the butter. Add the potatoes, bell pepper, carrots, and celery. Stir in the salt, onion powder, and pepper and cover the skillet. Cook for 5 minutes, stirring occasionally.

4. **Thicken it up.** Stir in the flour, combining it as best you can. Cook for 1 to 2 minutes. Pour in the vegetable broth and milk, stirring until the flour lumps are gone. Increase the heat to medium. Simmer for 4 to 5 minutes, or until the mixture thickens. Stir in the frozen peas and remove the skillet from the heat.

CONTINUED ▶

EQUIPMENT:

8-by-8-inch baking dish

Cutting board

Knife

Large skillet or pot

**Measuring cups
and spoons**

**Wooden spoon or
rubber/silicone spatula**

5. **Top the pie and bake.** Carefully pour the vegetable mixture into the prepared baking dish. Cover the top with the puff pastry, trimming it as needed so no more than ¼ inch of dough hangs over the edges of the baking dish. Cut 3 or 4 slits in the top to allow the steam from the hot veggies to escape, which prevents your puff pastry from getting too soggy. Bake for 15 minutes, or until the crust is a nice golden brown. Let cool for at least 5 minutes before serving.

Fun Fact: Not all premade puff pastries are vegan, but many are. Pepperidge Farm brand is what I call "accidentally vegan," which means it's not marketed as vegan, even though it is. It is available at most stores and is the brand I use.

Creamy Bacon and Pea Pasta

30 MINUTES / SERVES 4 / PREP TIME: 5 MINUTES / COOK TIME: 15 MINUTES

I remember when I first went vegan and thought I was giving up mac 'n' cheese forever. These days there are so many vegan cheese options—and that means no one has to go without mac 'n' cheese, which makes me very happy! Follow Your Heart and Daiya brands both make good vegan shredded cheeses. Check out the complete vegan cheese guide on page 8 for even more options.

INGREDIENTS:

8 ounces dried small pasta, such as shells or elbows

1½ cups shredded vegan cheddar cheese

1 cup nondairy milk

1 teaspoon yellow mustard

¼ teaspoon salt

⅛ teaspoon freshly ground black pepper

1 cup frozen peas

8 slices Baked Tempeh Bacon (page 24), chopped

EQUIPMENT:

1 large pot

1 medium saucepan or pot

Measuring cups and spoons

Rubber/silicone spatula

Colander

1. **Cook the pasta.** Bring a large pot of water to a boil. Add the pasta and cook according to the package directions.

2. **Make the sauce.** While the pasta cooks, heat a medium saucepan over medium heat. Add the cheddar, milk, mustard, salt, and pepper. Using a rubber spatula, stir so no cheese sticks to the sides of the pot. Cook for 5 to 6 minutes, stirring occasionally, or until the cheese melts and the sauce is thick and smooth. Stir in the frozen peas and the tempeh bacon, turn off the heat, cover the pot, and let sit for 1 to 2 minutes.

3. **Finish the dish.** Place a colander in the sink and drain the cooked pasta in it. Fold the pasta into the cheese sauce and serve.

Sloppy Joe Casserole

NUT-FREE, ONE POT / SERVES 6 / PREP TIME: 20 MINUTES / COOK TIME: 40 MINUTES

I remember eating sloppy Joe sandwiches at school when I was a kid, but I don't remember liking them very much! It wasn't until after I became vegan and started creating "veganized" versions of foods from my childhood that I realized how delicious sloppy Joes could be. I still enjoy them as sandwiches, but I love this casserole version best because crescent rolls (most brands of which are accidentally vegan) are one of my guilty pleasures.

INGREDIENTS:

Nonstick cooking spray

1 green bell pepper

1 Roma tomato

1 (15-ounce) can kidney beans

12 pickle chips

2 (8-count) tubes crescent roll dough (Pillsbury and many store brands are vegan; double-check the label)

4 tablespoons water, divided, plus more as needed

½ teaspoon onion powder

1 (15-ounce) can vegetarian refried beans

¼ cup quick-cooking oats

2 tablespoons spicy brown mustard

¼ teaspoon chili powder (optional)

1. **Turn on the oven and prep your baking dish.** Preheat the oven to 350°F. Lightly coat a 2-quart baking dish with cooking spray.

2. **Chop the veggies.** Dice the green bell pepper and tomato. Drain and rinse the kidney beans. Cut the pickle chips into quarters.

3. **Shape the crescent rolls.** Open the tubes of crescent rolls and roll them into their crescent shape, starting with the wider end of the triangle and rolling toward the narrow end. (I like to lay them out on a piece of parchment paper or aluminum foil.)

4. **Sauté and combine the ingredients.** In a nonstick skillet over medium heat, heat 2 tablespoons of water. Add the green bell pepper and onion powder. Cook for 2 to 3 minutes, or until the bell pepper just starts to soften. Add another tablespoon of water if the pan gets dry. Stir in the tomato, kidney beans, pickles, refried beans, oats, mustard, chili powder (if using), and remaining 2 tablespoons of water. Turn the heat to medium-high and let the mixture simmer for about 5 minutes, stirring often. You want it nice and hot without burning it on the bottom.

EQUIPMENT:

2-quart baking dish

Cutting board

Knife

Nonstick skillet

5. **Assemble and bake the casserole.** Spoon the sloppy Joe mixture into the prepared baking dish. Top with the crescent rolls, creating one nearly solid layer of doughy crescents. You may have to curve them a bit to fit. Bake, uncovered, for 20 to 30 minutes, until the crescent rolls are cooked through. You can lift the edge of one to check underneath (ask an adult for help). Let the casserole cool for 5 to 10 minutes before serving.

Getting Messy: All ovens are different, so don't worry if the casserole takes a little longer than 30 minutes to bake in your oven.

Baked Chickpea Burgers

NUT-FREE / SERVES 4 / PREP TIME: 10 MINUTES, PLUS 20 MINUTES TO CHILL /
COOK TIME: 25 MINUTES

I like to eat these chickpea burgers year-round, and because I live in Colorado, where winters are cold and snowy, that means I sometimes have to bake them. If you choose to grill or panfry them instead, line the grill grates or pan with a piece of oiled aluminum foil to prevent the burgers from falling apart. No matter how you cook them, I recommend serving with a side of fries and lots of toppings.

INGREDIENTS:

1 tablespoon chia seeds

2½ tablespoons water

1 (15-ounce) can chickpeas

½ bell pepper, any color

1 large carrot

1 teaspoon ground cumin

½ teaspoon salt

¼ teaspoon onion powder

¼ teaspoon freshly ground black pepper

½ cup bread crumbs

Nonstick cooking spray

4 whole-wheat burger buns

Optional toppings: lettuce, pickles, sliced tomato, ketchup, vegan mayo

1. **Mix your chia "egg."** In a small mixing bowl, stir together the chia seeds and water. Set aside. This creates an egg substitute called a "chia egg."

2. **Prepare the chickpeas and veggies.** Drain and rinse the chickpeas. Chop the bell pepper and carrot into large chunks.

3. **Blend.** In the food processor, combine the bell pepper and carrot pieces and pulse just until they are chopped into small chickpea-size pieces. Add the chickpeas and process on low speed for 5 to 10 seconds. A few whole beans are fine, but you want the majority to be blended—just not until it looks creamy like hummus.

4. **Finish the burger mixture and chill.** Using a rubber spatula, scrape the chickpea mixture into a medium mixing bowl and add the cumin, salt, onion powder, pepper, bread crumbs, and chia egg. Stir until well mixed, cover the bowl, and refrigerate for 20 minutes.

5. **Turn on the oven and prep your baking sheet.** Preheat the oven to 375°F. Lightly coat a large rimmed baking sheet with cooking spray.

CONTINUED ▶

EQUIPMENT:

Mixing bowls: 1 small, 1 medium

Measuring cups and spoons

Spoon

Cutting board

Knife

Food processor

Rubber/silicone spatula

Large rimmed baking sheet

6. **Cook the burgers.** Form the burger mixture into 4 equal patties and place them on the prepared baking sheet. Bake for 12 minutes. Flip the burgers and bake for 8 to 10 minutes more, or until they are lightly golden. Serve on buns with your favorite toppings.

Mix It Up: Like a little heat? Add ½ teaspoon of your favorite hot sauce in step 4!

Sweet 'n' Sour Tofu

GLUTEN-FREE, NUT-FREE / SERVES 4 / PREP TIME: 20 MINUTES / COOK TIME: 40 MINUTES

Sweet 'n' sour chicken was my favorite dish to order at Chinese restaurants when I was growing up—these days I order the tofu version. This version is easy to make and full of fresh vegetables.

INGREDIENTS:

Nonstick cooking spray

1 (14-ounce) block firm tofu, well pressed (see page 11)

½ sweet onion

1 green bell pepper

2 medium to large carrots

1 (8-ounce) can sliced water chestnuts

2 tablespoons water, plus more as needed

¾ cup jarred sweet and sour sauce, plus more as needed

2 cups cooked brown rice (either prepared in advance or microwavable, like Uncle Ben's)

EQUIPMENT:

Baking sheet

Aluminum foil

Cutting board

Knife

Tongs

Large skillet

Rubber/silicone spatula

1. **Turn on the oven and prep your baking sheet.** Preheat the oven to 420°F. Line a baking sheet with aluminum foil and lightly coat it with cooking spray.

2. **Bake the tofu.** Cut the tofu into bite-size cubes and place them on the prepared baking sheet in a single layer. Bake for 20 minutes. Remove the baking sheet from the oven and spritz the top of the tofu cubes with cooking spray. Using tongs, flip the cubes. Bake for 10 to 15 minutes more, or until the tofu is lightly golden brown and slightly puffy.

3. **Prepare the veggies.** Cut the onion and green bell pepper into bite-size chunks. Cut the carrots into thin circles (or half circles if the carrots are thick). Drain the water chestnuts and set aside.

4. **Cook the veggies and tofu.** In a large skillet over medium-low heat, heat the water. Add the onion, green bell pepper, and carrots. Sauté for 4 to 5 minutes, stirring, until just softened. Add another tablespoon of water if the pan gets dry. Add the tofu, sweet and sour sauce, and water chestnuts. Simmer for 4 to 5 minutes until everything is warmed through. Depending on the sauce you use, you may need to add an additional ¼ cup or so. You want it saucy, but not soupy. Serve over cooked brown rice.

Mix It Up: This dish is perfect for adding more veggies . . . and even fruit! Pineapple chunks (canned in juice, not syrup, are the healthiest and most delicious), snap peas, celery—whatever your favorite is!

Spaghetti and Beanballs

NUT-FREE / SERVES 4 / PREP TIME: 15 MINUTES / COOK TIME: 45 MINUTES

This was one of my favorite meals when I was a kid. Guess what? It still is! The only difference is that now I use beanballs. They're yummy to eat and fun to make because you get to use your hands. An easy way to make sure your beanballs are all the same size is to divide the bean mixture in half and then in half again, so you have four even sections. Then, make three balls from each section, and they'll all be about the same size.

FOR THE BEANBALLS:

Nonstick cooking spray

1 (15-ounce) can
kidney beans

¼ cup bread crumbs

2 teaspoons olive oil

2 teaspoons
Italian seasoning

½ teaspoon onion powder

¼ teaspoon freshly
squeezed lemon juice

¼ teaspoon salt

¼ teaspoon red pepper
flakes (optional)

2 teaspoons
water (optional)

FOR THE SPAGHETTI:

Pinch salt

8 ounces dried spaghetti
(regular or angel hair)

1 (24-ounce) jar your
favorite pasta sauce

Optional: Fresh basil,
for topping

1. **Turn on the oven and prep your baking sheet.** Preheat the oven to 375°F. Coat a large rimmed baking sheet with cooking spray.

2. **Mash the beans and add seasonings.** Drain and rinse the kidney beans. Pour the beans into a large mixing bowl and mash with a potato masher or the back of a fork. Make sure most of the beans are smashed (although, some bigger pieces are okay). Add the bread crumbs, olive oil, Italian seasoning, onion powder, lemon juice, salt, and red pepper flakes (if using). Using your (clean) hands, mix everything to combine.

3. **Roll the beanballs.** Still using your hands, roll the bean mixture into 12 identical balls, making sure you squeeze them tight and round. If the mixture isn't sticking together, add the water, 1 teaspoon at a time, and mix it in, then try again.

4. **Bake the beanballs.** Place the beanballs on the prepared baking sheet at least 1 inch apart and give them a light spritz with cooking spray. Bake for 20 minutes. Turn the beanballs over, spritz again with cooking spray, and bake for 15 to 20 minutes more, or until they're nice and golden.

CONTINUED ▶

EQUIPMENT:

**Large rimmed
baking sheet**

Large mixing bowl

Potato masher or fork

**Measuring cups
and spoons**

Large pot

Pasta spoon

Colander

5. **Cook the pasta.** While the beanballs bake, bring a large pot containing 4 to 6 quarts water to a rolling boil over high heat. Add the salt, and then the spaghetti. Stir gently with your pasta spoon until the pasta softens enough that it is covered by the water. Return to a boil and cook the pasta for 9 to 10 minutes for regular spaghetti, or 4 to 5 minutes for angel hair. Stir gently every couple of minutes. When you think the pasta is done, use the pasta spoon to pull out one strand. Let it cool for a few moments, then bite into it to make sure it's done. If it's crunchy, it isn't done and needs to cook longer. Check again in another minute. If it's slightly firm or just barely soft, it is done!

6. **Combine the pasta, sauce, and beanballs.** Turn off the heat. Place a colander in the sink and drain the pasta in it (ask an adult for help and watch out for the hot steam). Return the pasta to the pot and stir in the pasta sauce. Add the beanballs and gently stir so they don't break apart too much. Cover the pot and let sit for 5 minutes. Using your pasta spoon or tongs, scoop the spaghetti into bowls and top with basil (if using).

Mix It Up: To make this recipe gluten free, use gluten-free panko bread crumbs in the beanballs and gluten-free pasta.

Korean-Inspired Barbecue Bowls

5-INGREDIENT, GLUTEN-FREE, NUT-FREE / SERVES 4 / PREP TIME: 15 MINUTES / COOK TIME: 35 MINUTES

I have a friend I've known since middle school who is from South Korea and she's taught me a lot about Korean ingredients and flavors. Although this is definitely not a traditional dish, it does incorporate delicious Korean barbecue sauce, which I love. Most grocery stores carry this premade sauce in their international aisles.

INGREDIENTS:

Nonstick cooking spray

1 (14-ounce) block firm tofu, well pressed (see page 11)

1 red bell pepper

2 tablespoons water, plus more as needed

4 rounded cups broccoli florets

¾ cup bottled Korean barbecue sauce

2 cups cooked brown rice (either prepared in advance or microwavable, like Uncle Ben's)

EQUIPMENT:

Baking sheet

Aluminum foil

Cutting board

Knife

Measuring cups and spoons

Large skillet

1. **Turn on the oven and prep your baking sheet.** Preheat the oven to 420°F. Line a baking sheet with aluminum foil and lightly coat it with cooking spray. Set aside.

2. **Bake the tofu.** Cut the tofu into bite-size cubes. Place them on the prepared baking sheet in a single layer. Bake for 20 minutes. Remove the baking sheet from the oven and spritz the top of the tofu cubes with cooking spray. Using tongs, flip the cubes. Bake for 10 to 15 minutes more, or until the tofu is lightly golden brown and slightly puffy.

3. **Cook the veggies.** Cut the red bell pepper into large dice (about ½ inch). In a large skillet over medium-low heat, heat the water. Add the red bell pepper and broccoli. Cover the skillet and simmer for 2 to 3 minutes, stirring occasionally, adding an additional tablespoon of water if the pan dries out.

4. **Add the flavor.** Stir in the tofu and barbecue sauce. Simmer for 5 minutes, uncovered. Serve in bowls over the cooked brown rice.

Cauliflower 'n' Cheese

NUT-FREE / SERVES 4 / PREP TIME: 15 MINUTES / COOK TIME: 30 MINUTES

The only vegetables I really liked when I was a kid were carrots, peas, and corn, but I think that if my mom had made me this cauliflower dish, I would've loved it! This recipe makes a great meal all on its own, but it's also the perfect side dish for Baked Chickpea Burgers (page 91). Keep in mind that it makes six servings as a side dish.

INGREDIENTS:

Nonstick cooking spray

Salt

1 large head cauliflower

2 cups shredded vegan cheddar cheese

1½ cups unsweetened oat milk

½ teaspoon garlic powder

½ teaspoon onion powder

⅛ teaspoon freshly ground black pepper

1½ cups panko bread crumbs

½ teaspoon paprika

Optional: 2 tablespoons chopped fresh parsley

EQUIPMENT:

1½-quart baking dish

2 medium saucepans

Cutting board

Knife

Colander

Paper towel

Rubber/silicone spatula

1. **Turn on the oven and prep your baking dish.** Preheat the oven to 350°F. Lightly coat a 1½-quart baking dish with cooking spray. Set aside.

2. **Boil the water.** Bring a medium saucepan full of salted water to a boil over high heat.

3. **Prep and parboil the cauliflower.** Using a sharp knife, cut the cauliflower into bite-size pieces (ask an adult for help if you need it). You should have about 8 cups of small florets. Carefully drop the cauliflower into the boiling water and cook for about 5 minutes, until just slightly soft (this is called parboiling). Place a colander in the sink and drain the cauliflower in it. Pat the cauliflower dry with paper towel.

4. **Make the cheese sauce.** In another medium saucepan over medium heat, combine the cheddar, milk, garlic powder, onion powder, ¼ teaspoon salt, and pepper. Cook for 5 to 6 minutes, stirring occasionally, until the cheese is completely melted. A rubber spatula is great for making sure no cheese sticks to the sides of the pan.

5. **Combine and bake.** Fold the drained cauliflower into the cheese sauce, then pour the entire mixture into the prepared baking dish. Cover with the bread crumbs and sprinkle with the paprika. Bake for 15 to 20 minutes. If you'd like the top to be a little more golden brown, after the cauliflower is done baking, turn the broiler to low heat and broil for about 30 seconds, or until the top of the casserole is crispy, watching it closely. Top with parsley (if using) and serve.

Spicy Peanut Noodles

30 MINUTES, GLUTEN-FREE, ONE POT / SERVES 4 / PREP TIME: 15 MINUTES / COOK TIME: 15 MINUTES

Don't let the name of this dish scare you—it isn't really that spicy. At least, not unless you want it to be! The chili sauce works well with the sweet and salty flavors of the peanut butter, combining so that no one flavor is the strongest. I like adding the peanuts as a topping before serving—they add a fun crunch (as well as protein)!

FOR THE SAUCE:

½ cup creamy peanut butter

2 tablespoons rice vinegar

1 tablespoon gluten-free low-sodium soy sauce

1 teaspoon chili sauce (like sriracha), plus more for seasoning

¼ teaspoon ground ginger

Juice of ½ lime (cut the other half into wedges for serving)

¼ cup hot water

FOR THE NOODLES:

8 ounces rice noodles

1 red bell pepper

½ cucumber

1 large carrot

2 tablespoons water, plus more for cooking the noodles

Optional: ¼ cup roasted chopped peanuts

¼ cup sliced scallions (optional)

1. **Make the sauce.** In a small mixing bowl, whisk the peanut butter, vinegar, soy sauce, chili sauce, ginger, lime juice, and hot water until smooth. Taste and add more chili sauce, if desired. Set aside.

2. **Cook the rice noodles.** Bring a large pot of water to a boil over high heat. Add the noodles and cook according to the package directions (they generally need to be boiled for 4 to 6 minutes), until they are tender but still firm. Place a colander in the sink and drain the noodles in it. Rinse the noodles well with cold water.

3. **Prep your veggies.** Slice the red bell pepper into thin strips, about 1 inch long. Halve the cucumber lengthwise, then cut it into thin half-moons. Cut the carrot into thin circles (or half circles, if it's thick).

**Measuring cups
and spoons**

Small mixing bowl

Whisk

Large pot

Colander

Cutting board

Knife

Large skillet

Rubber/silicone spatula

4. **Finish the veggies and noodles.** In a large skillet over medium heat, heat the water. Add the red bell pepper, cucumber, and carrot. Sauté for 2 to 3 minutes, then stir in the noodles and peanut sauce. Reduce the heat to low and let sit, uncovered, for 2 to 3 minutes, stirring occasionally. Serve topped with peanuts and scallion (if using) and with lime wedges on the side for squeezing.

Mix It Up: Want to feed a couple extra people with this recipe? Add baked tofu, using the instructions from Korean-Inspired Barbecue Bowls on page 97.

Coconut Curry Bowls

30 MINUTES, GLUTEN-FREE, ONE POT / SERVES 4 / PREP TIME: 15 MINUTES / COOK TIME: 15 MINUTES

Please don't tell the other recipes in this book, but this one is my favorite! It's so creamy and rich, yet it doesn't take very long to make. There are so many different curries out there from many different parts of the world, and I encourage you to experiment with all of them—but this simple curry is a good place to start.

INGREDIENTS:

2 large carrots

1 (15-ounce) can great northern beans

¼ cup water, plus 2 teaspoons, plus more as needed

3 heaping cups broccoli florets

1 (15-ounce) can light coconut milk

2 teaspoons red curry paste

½ teaspoon salt

2 teaspoons cornstarch

4 cups frozen cauliflower rice

EQUIPMENT:

Cutting board

Knife

Large skillet

Spoon

Small mixing bowl

Small whisk

1. **Prep the ingredients.** Cut the carrots into thin circles. Drain and rinse the great northern beans.

2. **Cook the veggies.** In a large skillet over medium-low heat, heat ¼ cup of water. Add the carrots and broccoli. Simmer for 3 to 4 minutes, stirring occasionally, adding an additional tablespoon of water if the pan gets dry.

3. **Combine the flavors.** Stir in the great northern beans, coconut milk, red curry paste, and salt. In a small mixing bowl, whisk the cornstarch with the remaining 2 teaspoons of water, then add this slurry to the skillet. Increase the heat to high and cook until the sauce begins to boil. Reduce the heat to low and simmer for about 5 minutes, or until the sauce thickens and the veggies are tender.

4. **Prepare the cauliflower rice and serve.** While the curry simmers, cook the cauliflower rice according to the package instructions. (Some brands differ, but many are in microwavable bags and only take a couple minutes to cook.) Divide the rice among 4 bowls and top with the curry.

Peanut Butter–Coconut Cookies, page 106

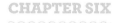

DESSERTS AND TREATS

Peanut Butter–Coconut Cookies

30 MINUTES / SERVES 10 (MAKES 20 COOKIES) / PREP TIME: 20 MINUTES / COOK TIME: 14 MINUTES

I grew up eating a lot of peanut butter, mostly in sandwiches, which isn't nearly as much fun as eating it in cookies. Coconut is one of my favorite flavors, so I added some to make these cookies extra special. I love packing one in my lunch for a midday treat or crumbling one or two over a bowl of ice cream for dessert.

INGREDIENTS:

1½ cups all-purpose flour

¼ cup unsweetened shredded coconut

1 teaspoon baking powder

1 teaspoon baking soda

½ cup vegan butter, at room temperature

½ cup granulated sugar

½ cup packed light brown sugar

1 cup creamy peanut butter

1 tablespoon vanilla extract

1 tablespoon unsweetened nondairy milk, plus more as needed (optional; depending on the peanut butter you use, this may not be necessary)

1. **Turn on the oven and prep your baking sheet.** Preheat the oven to 375°F. Line a baking sheet with parchment paper.

2. **Combine the dry ingredients.** In a small mixing bowl, stir together the flour, coconut, baking powder, and baking soda. Set aside.

3. **Combine the wet ingredients.** In the bowl of a stand mixer or a large mixing bowl using a handheld electric mixer, combine the butter, granulated sugar, and brown sugar. Cream together on medium speed for 2 to 3 minutes. Add the peanut butter and vanilla and mix just until combined. Slowly add the dry ingredients to the wet ingredients, stirring by hand until well mixed.

4. **Check your dough.** Try rolling a tablespoon of the dough into a ball. If it sticks together, your dough is ready. If it's dry and crumbly, stir in 1 tablespoon of nondairy milk, then try again. Repeat until you're able to roll a mostly smooth ball of dough.

5. **Shape and bake the cookies.** Use a tablespoon to portion the cookie dough. Using your (clean) hands, roll each portion into a ball and place it on the prepared baking sheet. Using the back of a fork,

Baking sheet

Parchment paper

Measuring cups or spoons

Small mixing bowl

Spoon

Stand mixer with paddle attachment or large mixing bowl and handheld electric mixer

Fork

Flat turning spatula

Wire rack

flatten the cookies, creating a crisscross pattern. Bake for 10 to 14 minutes, or until the edges are set and the tops are golden brown. Let cool on the baking sheet for 5 to 6 minutes, then use a turning spatula to move them to a wire rack to cool for 10 minutes more.

Getting Messy: Wondering why you may or may not need to add milk to the dough? Some peanut butter brands have more moisture than others. By waiting to add the milk, you can avoid the dough becoming too moist and then spreading too much during baking.

Chocolate Chip Cookies

SERVES 10 (MAKES 20 COOKIES) / PREP TIME: 25 MINUTES / COOK TIME: 15 MINUTES

Back when I first went vegan, there were no plant-based cookies at the grocery store. If I wanted cookies, I had to make my own. Nowadays there are plenty of vegan store-bought cookie options but, when it comes to a classic like chocolate chip cookies, I still think homemade is best . . . mostly because it's the only way you get to enjoy a soft, still-warm cookie with a glass of your favorite nondairy milk any time you want!

INGREDIENTS:

½ cup vegan butter, at room temperature

1 cup packed light brown sugar

¼ cup unsweetened nondairy milk

1 tablespoon vanilla extract

2 cups all-purpose flour

2 teaspoons cornstarch

1 teaspoon baking powder

1 teaspoon baking soda

¼ teaspoon ground cinnamon

¼ teaspoon salt

1 cup vegan chocolate chips

1. **Turn on the oven and prep your baking sheet.** Preheat the oven to 350°F. Line a baking sheet with parchment paper. Set aside.

2. **Mix the wet ingredients.** In the bowl of a stand mixer or a large mixing bowl using a handheld electric mixer, combine the butter and brown sugar. Cream together on medium speed for 2 to 3 minutes. Add the milk and vanilla and mix just until smooth.

3. **Mix the dry ingredients.** In a small mixing bowl, whisk the flour, cornstarch, baking powder, baking soda, cinnamon, and salt until completely mixed.

4. **Combine.** Slowly add the dry ingredients to the wet ingredients and mix. I like to use the paddle attachment, as it keeps anything from sticking to the sides of the bowl. Stir just until completely mixed, then stir in the chocolate chips.

5. **Shape and bake the cookies.** Now you get to use your (clean) hands! In the bowl, divide the cookie dough in half, then into quarters. This will help make sure your cookies are the same size. Divide each quarter into 5 pieces (you'll have 20 dough pieces), then roll the dough into balls. Place the

**Large rimmed
baking sheet**

Parchment paper

Whisk

**Stand mixer with paddle
attachment or large
mixing bowl and handheld
electric mixer**

Rubber/silicone spatula

Small mixing bowl

Whisk

Flat turning spatula

Wire rack

cookie balls on the prepared baking sheet. Bake for 13 to 15 minutes, or until the tops are slightly golden brown. Remove from the oven and let cool for 5 minutes, then transfer them to a wire rack to cool completely.

Mix It Up: Vegan chocolate chunks, which are larger than chips, are a fun way to change up these cookies. Or try vegan white chocolate chips or chunks.

Baked Cinnamon Sugar Donuts

SERVES 6 (MAKES 12 DONUTS) / PREP TIME: 25 MINUTES / COOK TIME: 16 MINUTES

The smell of fresh donuts is one of the very best smells in the world! Sweet and rich … you can almost taste these donuts as they're coming out of the oven (but not yet! They're still hot!). I remember my dad making donuts on a weekend morning when I was young. His donuts were cooked in oil on the stovetop, and as much as I enjoyed those heavenly treats, this version is healthier and easier to make. If you have a donut pan, great! Your treats will come out looking like mini versions of bakery donuts. You can also use a muffin tin. The donuts won't have a hole in the center, but they'll taste just as scrumptious!

FOR THE DONUTS:

Nonstick cooking spray

1½ cups all-purpose flour

½ cup granulated sugar

¼ cup packed light brown sugar

2 teaspoons baking powder

½ teaspoon ground cinnamon

¼ teaspoon salt

¾ cup unsweetened nondairy milk

5 tablespoons melted coconut oil

2 tablespoons unsweetened applesauce

1½ teaspoons vanilla extract

1. **Turn on the oven and prep your donut trays.** Preheat the oven to 350°F. Lightly coat 2 (6-count) donut trays or 2 (6-cup) muffin tins with cooking spray.

2. **Mix the batter.** In a large mixing bowl, whisk the flour, granulated sugar, brown sugar, baking powder, cinnamon, and salt. Add the milk, melted coconut oil, applesauce, and vanilla. Whisk well to combine and break up any lumps.

3. **Pour the batter into the trays and bake.** If you are using a mixing bowl with a spout, carefully pour the batter into the prepared trays. If not, use a large spoon to fill the trays with batter. (Ask an adult for help, if needed.) Bake for 14 to 15 minutes, or until the donuts are light golden brown on top.

4. **Let cool.** Let the donuts cool in the trays for a few minutes, then transfer the donuts to a wire rack to cool completely.

CONTINUED ▸

FOR THE TOPPING:

**2 tablespoons
vegan butter**

½ cup granulated sugar

**1 teaspoon
ground cinnamon**

EQUIPMENT:

**Large mixing bowl,
preferably a batter bowl
with a spout for pouring**

Whisk

**2 (6-count) donut trays or
2 (6-cup) muffin tins**

Spoon

Wire rack

**2 wide shallow bowls
(1 microwave-safe)**

5. **Prepare the cinnamon sugar topping.** In a wide, shallow, microwave-safe bowl, melt the butter in the microwave on High power, just a few seconds at a time, stirring between each cooking time. Ask an adult for help with this. In a second bowl, stir together the granulated sugar and cinnamon.

6. **Decorate the donuts.** Holding each donut upside-down, just barely dip it into the melted butter for just a second, then dip it into the cinnamon sugar. Repeat for each donut, then line the donuts up on a tray and sprinkle the remaining cinnamon sugar over the tops.

Spiced Vanilla Pudding

5-INGREDIENT, ONE POT / SERVES 4 / PREP TIME: 5 MINUTES /
COOK TIME: 10 MINUTES, PLUS 2 HOURS TO CHILL

Vanilla pudding is a simple, easy dessert . . . but this version has a little twist—nutmeg! This unexpected spice adds just a hint of flavor that makes this pudding better than all the other puddings (in my opinion, anyway). It's perfect on its own, and even better topped with some sliced fresh fruit.

INGREDIENTS:

⅓ cup sugar

¼ cup cornstarch

¼ teaspoon salt

2 cups unsweetened nondairy milk

1 teaspoon vanilla extract

⅛ teaspoon ground nutmeg

EQUIPMENT:

Small or medium saucepan or pot

Whisk

Rubber/silicone spatula

Medium mixing bowl

Plastic wrap

1. **Mix the dry ingredients.** In a small or medium saucepan or pot, whisk the sugar, cornstarch, and salt to combine.

2. **Add the milk and begin to cook.** Pour in the milk and whisk until completely blended. Place the pan over medium-low heat and cook, stirring constantly, for 2 to 3 minutes, just until you start to see a bit of steam rising. Reduce the heat to low.

3. **Continue to cook.** Switch to a rubber spatula and cook for 2 to 3 minutes more, stirring constantly, or until the pudding thickens. The spatula will help ensure nothing is stuck to the sides or bottom of the pan.

4. **Add the final seasonings and chill.** Remove the pan from heat and stir in the vanilla and nutmeg. Let cool for 8 to 10 minutes, stirring occasionally. Pour the pudding into a medium mixing bowl and place a layer of plastic wrap directly on the top of the pudding. When the pudding is exposed to air in the refrigerator, the very top will form a thin layer that is a different texture. It's edible, but nicer without it. The plastic wrap will help keep this "skin" from forming. Chill for 2 hours, or until completely firm.

PB&J Ice Cream Pie

5-INGREDIENT, ONE POT / **SERVES 6** / **PREP TIME: 20 MINUTES, PLUS 2 HOURS TO CHILL**

Ice cream pies are the easiest pies to make because there's no baking required. This pie can be made in advance and taken out of the freezer to soften a few minutes before you're ready to eat it. And, in case you don't love raspberries, any preserves will work. Use the one you most enjoy on your PB&J sandwiches!

INGREDIENTS:

1 quart no-sugar-added vegan vanilla ice cream

½ cup creamy peanut butter

1 (9-inch) vegan graham cracker piecrust (such as Keebler)

½ cup raspberry preserves

EQUIPMENT:

Large mixing bowl

Rubber/silicone spatula

Handheld electric mixer

Spoon

Aluminum foil or plastic wrap

1. **Blend the ice cream and peanut butter.** Let the ice cream sit on the counter for 5 to 10 minutes, or until softened enough to scoop it out of the container. In a large mixing bowl, combine the softened ice cream and peanut butter. Using a handheld electric mixer, mix on low speed until smooth.

2. **Start layering the pie.** Pour the ice cream mixture into the piecrust and smooth the top with the back of a spoon. Loosely cover the pie with aluminum foil or plastic wrap and place the pie in the freezer for 1 hour, or until the pie is firm enough to hold the preserves on top.

3. **Add the preserves.** Pour the preserves on top of the pie. Using the back of a spoon, gently spread the preserves into an even layer. Re-cover the pie and return it to the freezer for at least 1 hour, or until solid.

Getting Messy: Because the ice cream layer has peanut butter in it, it will freeze harder than ice cream normally does. This means you need to let the pie sit out for about 5 minutes before you'll be able to enjoy it.

Cookies 'n' Cream Cake

ONE POT / SERVES 8 / PREP TIME: 25 MINUTES / COOK TIME: 45 MINUTES

This chocolate cake is extra easy to make because you don't have to frost it—just slice and serve with a big dollop of whipped coconut topping PLUS cookies.

INGREDIENTS:

Nonstick cooking spray

1½ cups all-purpose flour

½ cup granulated sugar

½ cup packed light brown sugar

¼ cup cocoa powder

1 teaspoon baking soda

½ teaspoon salt

1 cup unsweetened nondairy milk

⅓ cup unsweetened applesauce

1½ teaspoons vanilla extract

1 teaspoon apple cider vinegar

8 vegan chocolate sandwich cookies (like Newman-O's or Oreos)

8 ounces whipped coconut topping (such as So Delicious Cocowhip)

EQUIPMENT:

9-by-5-inch loaf pan

Mixing bowls: 1 large, 1 medium

Whisk

Rubber/silicone spatula

Wire rack

Cutting board

Knife

1. **Turn on the oven and prep your cake pan.** Preheat the oven to 350°F. Lightly coat the inside of a 9-by-5 loaf pan with cooking spray. Set aside.

2. **Mix the dry ingredients.** In a large mixing bowl, whisk the flour, granulated sugar, brown sugar, cocoa powder, baking soda, and salt to combine well.

3. **Mix the wet ingredients, then combine.** In a medium mixing bowl, stir together the milk, applesauce, vanilla, and vinegar. Slowly add the wet ingredients to the dry ingredients, stirring as you go. A rubber spatula works great for this step!

4. **Bake.** Pour the batter into the prepared pan. Bake on the center rack for 40 to 45 minutes, or until the sides of the cake have begun to pull away from the pan. You can also stick a toothpick into the center of the cake; if it comes out clean, the cake is done! Transfer the cake to a wire rack and let it cool in the pan. If you need it to cool quickly, refrigerate it.

5. **Chop the cookies.** Roughly chop the cookies into quarters. They will break apart a bit, but that's okay because you're sprinkling them on top!

6. **Finish and serve.** Slice the cooled cake and serve with the whipped topping spread evenly over the top and sprinkled with the cookies. I like to sprinkle them evenly over the Cocowhip.

Mix It Up: Try breaking the cake up into small pieces and freezing them in an airtight container, then mixing them with your favorite vegan ice cream!

Apple Crisp

NUT-FREE / SERVES 6 / PREP TIME: 25 MINUTES / COOK TIME: 40 MINUTES

Baked goods with apples, cinnamon, and nutmeg always remind me of autumn but, the truth is, they're good year-round. Choose crisp, juicy apples (like Honeycrisp or Fuji or, if you want something tart, Granny Smith) that will hold up well during baking. I like to include a mix of two or three different kinds of apples to give the crisp extra flavor. Although this crisp is wonderful by itself, consider serving it with a scoop of your favorite vegan vanilla ice cream.

INGREDIENTS:

Nonstick cooking spray

5 apples

3 tablespoons granulated sugar

1 teaspoon ground cinnamon

¼ teaspoon salt

⅛ teaspoon ground nutmeg

¾ cup old-fashioned rolled oats

¾ cup all-purpose flour

½ cup packed light brown sugar

½ teaspoon vanilla extract

5 tablespoons vegan butter

1. **Turn on the oven and prep your baking dish.** Preheat the oven to 375°F. Lightly coat a 9-inch square baking dish with cooking spray. Set aside.

2. **Peel and slice the apples.** Peel the apples, then cut the apple away from the core: Hold the apple stem-side up on the cutting board and cut off one side, leaving the core. Cut off another side, leaving the core. Do this 2 more times to remove the rest of the apple, leaving just the core. Repeat with the remaining 4 apples. Cut the apples into thin slices, being careful to keep the thickness of your slices the same.

3. **Mix the filling.** In a large mixing bowl, stir together the apples, granulated sugar, cinnamon, salt, and nutmeg, stirring until the apple pieces are coated. Pour the apples into the prepared baking dish.

4. **Mix the topping.** In a medium mixing bowl, stir together the oats, flour, brown sugar, and vanilla extract. In a small microwave-safe bowl, melt the butter in the microwave on High power, just a few seconds at a time, stirring between each cooking time. (Ask an adult for help with this.) Stir the melted butter into the oat mixture until it's evenly moistened.

9-inch square baking dish

Peeler

Cutting board

Knife

Mixing bowls: 1 large, 1 medium

Spoon

Small microwave-safe bowl

5. **Add the topping and bake.** Spoon the oat topping over the filling in the baking dish in an even layer. Bake for 35 to 40 minutes (asking an adult to rotate the dish once about halfway through baking time), or until the filling is bubbly and the top is golden brown. Let cool before serving.

Mix It Up: Try substituting a Bartlett or Bosc pear for one or two of the apples. This makes it especially fun when your family is enjoying the crisp and trying to figure out what that wonderful flavor is!

Salted Caramel Sundaes

5-INGREDIENT, ONE POT / SERVES 4 / PREP TIME: 10 MINUTES / COOK TIME: 1 HOUR, PLUS 1 HOUR AT ROOM TEMPERATURE AND OVERNIGHT TO CHILL

Caramel was always my favorite sundae topping when I was a kid, and I thought going vegan meant giving it up forever because it is traditionally made with dairy. For a while, that did seem to be the case, but then I learned how easy it is to make my own caramel from canned coconut milk. There is a lot of stirring involved and some waiting for the flavors to deepen and the texture to be just right, but it is totally worth it. This sauce is so rich and creamy and *salty* . . . I can't get enough!

FOR THE CARAMEL SAUCE:

1 (13.5-ounce) can full-fat coconut milk

⅓ cup real maple syrup

¼ cup packed light brown sugar

½ teaspoon vanilla extract

1 teaspoon sea salt

FOR THE SUNDAES:

1 pint vegan vanilla ice cream

Optional toppings: coconut whipped cream, sprinkles, cherries

EQUIPMENT:

Medium saucepan

Rubber/silicone spatula

1. **Make the caramel sauce.** In a medium saucepan over high heat, combine the coconut milk, maple syrup, and brown sugar. Cook, stirring occasionally with a rubber spatula, until the mixture begins to boil. Cook for about 3 minutes, stirring continuously now.

2. **Reduce the caramel.** Reduce the heat to low and let the sauce simmer, stirring occasionally, for 45 to 50 minutes, or until the sauce has cooked down by about half and is nice and thick. Remove from the heat and stir in the vanilla. Let sit at room temperature for 45 minutes to 1 hour to thicken. Stir in the salt, cover the pan, and refrigerate for at least 8 hours, but overnight is best. This allows the flavor to deepen and the sauce to thicken completely.

3. **Build the sundaes.** Scoop the ice cream into 4 serving bowls and top with the cooled caramel sauce and any toppings you like.

Mix It Up: Try these sundaes with chocolate ice cream, or any other flavor you like.

MEASUREMENT CONVERSIONS

VOLUME EQUIVALENTS (LIQUID)

US STANDARD	US STANDARD (OUNCES)	METRIC (APPROXIMATE)
2 tablespoons	1 fl. oz.	30 mL
¼ cup	2 fl. oz.	60 mL
½ cup	4 fl. oz.	120 mL
1 cup	8 fl. oz.	240 mL
1½ cups	12 fl. oz.	355 mL
2 cups or 1 pint	16 fl. oz.	475 mL
4 cups or 1 quart	32 fl. oz.	1 L
1 gallon	128 fl. oz.	4 L

OVEN TEMPERATURES

FAHRENHEIT	CELSIUS (APPROXIMATE)
250°F	120°C
300°F	150°C
325°F	165°C
350°F	180°C
375°F	190°C
400°F	200°C
425°F	220°C
450°F	230°C

VOLUME EQUIVALENTS (DRY)

US STANDARD	METRIC (APPROXIMATE)
⅛ teaspoon	0.5 mL
¼ teaspoon	1 mL
½ teaspoon	2 mL
¾ teaspoon	4 mL
1 teaspoon	5 mL
1 tablespoon	15 mL
¼ cup	59 mL
⅓ cup	79 mL
½ cup	118 mL
⅔ cup	156 mL
¾ cup	177 mL
1 cup	235 mL
2 cups or 1 pint	475 mL
3 cups	700 mL
4 cups or 1 quart	1 L

WEIGHT EQUIVALENTS

US STANDARD	METRIC (APPROXIMATE)
½ ounce	15 g
1 ounce	30 g
2 ounces	60 g
4 ounces	115 g
8 ounces	225 g
12 ounces	340 g
16 ounces or 1 pound	455 g

RESOURCES

FOR PARENTS AND OTHER ADULT HELPERS

Here's a list of handy tools, stores, and websites that will help your kid chef learn and grow in the kitchen.

THE BEST CHILD-SAFE KNIVES AND CHOPPERS

Kitchen safety is very important and, luckily, there are quite a few knives on the market designed for young chefs. Most come in multiple sizes to accommodate growing hands.

Nylon knives With nylon, serrated blades and dull tips, these knives can help kids learn to cut and chop even tough fruits and veggies.

Safety knives For older kids, you might consider knives with metal blades designed to be dull. These can teach knife skills and grip, but are still safe.

"Slap" choppers These handheld and countertop tools allow you to chop and dice without having to hold a blade. They could also be a good option for children who are unable to finely dice.

WHERE TO FIND VEGAN FOODS

These days, most grocery stores carry a plethora of vegan alternatives, but if you're having trouble finding particular items, I recommend checking your local health food store or cooperative and chains like Sprouts, Natural Grocers, and Whole Foods. Asian markets tend to have a wide variety of vegan options as well. There are also online retailers that carry nearly every vegan ingredient ever made, like VeganEssentials.com, BillionVegans.com, and, of course, Amazon.com.

INDEX

ACKNOWLEDGMENTS

Thank you to everyone who took the time to answer my (sometimes silly) questions about the recipes kids like to cook, the vegetables they probably won't eat, and if there really is such a thing as too much sugar. (Spoiler alert: The answer is no.)

As always, thank you Denise Lindom for your food-related wisdom and your willingness to indulge my love of cheap sangria. That is truly what friends are for. A million thank-yous to my recipe testers who took the time to help make this book great: Susan and Erin Burgmaier, Brooke and Maddie Dunn, Shawna, Gabe, and Anna Karlson, and Cynthia Thayer. I'm so grateful for your help!

Last, but definitely not least, thank you to my editors Bridget Fitzgerald and Myryah Irby who make everything seem easy, and to all the wonderful folks at Callisto Media!

ABOUT THE AUTHOR

 **Barb Musick** lives in Colorado with her pack of rescue pets. She shares her adventures and love of food, travel, and animals on her blog, *That Was Vegan?*, along with vegan recipes everyone will love. Visit her at ThatWasVegan.com.

CPSIA information can be obtained
at www.ICGtesting.com
Printed in the USA
BVHW050742121120
592869BV00004B/7